SPIRITUAL
PERSPECTIVES
ON
AMERICA'S ROLE
AS SUPERPOWER

Contributors:

Dr. Beatrice Bruteau

Rev. Dr. Joan Brown Campbell

Tony Campolo

Rev. Forrest Church

Lama Surya Das

Matthew Fox

Kabir Helminski

Thich Nhat Hanh

Eboo Patel

Abbot M. Basil Pennington, OSCO

Dennis Prager

Rosemary Radford Ruether

Wayne Teasdale

Rev. William McD. Tully

Rabbi Arthur Waskow

John Wilson

SPIRITUAL PERSPECTIVES

ON

AMERICA'S ROLE AS SUPERPOWER

Created by the Editors at SkyLight Paths

Walking Together, Finding the Way
SKYLIGHT PATHS Publishing
Woodstock, Vermont

Spiritual Perspectives on America's Role as Superpower

2003 Second Printing
2003 First Printing
© 2003 by SkyLight Paths Publishing

Library of Congress Cataloging-in-Publication Data
Spiritual perspectives on America's role as superpower / created by the editors at SkyLight Paths; contributors: Beatrice Bruteau ... [et al.].
     p. cm.
Includes bibliographical references.
ISBN 1-893361-81-0 (quality pbk.)
1. Religion and international affairs. 2. Religion and politics—United States. 3. United States—Foreign relations—Moral and ethical aspects. I. Bruteau, Beatrice, 1930– II. SkyLight Paths Publishing.
BL65.I55S68 2003
291.1'787'0973—dc21
                                  2003000845

Page 229 constitutes a continuation of this copyright page.

10   9   8   7   6   5   4   3   2

Manufactured in the United States of America

SkyLight Paths Publishing is creating a place where people of different spiritual traditions come together for challenge and inspiration, a place where we can help each other understand the mystery that lies at the heart of our existence.

SkyLight Paths sees both believers and seekers as a community that increasingly transcends traditional boundaries of religion and denomination—people wanting to learn from each other, *walking together, finding the way.*

SkyLight Paths, "Walking Together, Finding the Way" and colophon are trademarks of LongHill Partners, Inc., registered in the U.S. Patent and Trademark Office.

Walking Together, Finding the Way
Published by SkyLight Paths Publishing
A Division of LongHill Partners, Inc.
Sunset Farm Offices, Route 4, P.O. Box 237
Woodstock, VT 05091
Tel: (802) 457-4000   Fax: (802) 457-4004
www.skylightpaths.com

Contents

Introduction

Difficult issues are debated each day in our seats of government and in the media. The op-ed pages, talk shows, radio commentaries, telecasts of congressional debates on C-Span—all of these voices are clamoring to be heard. But frequently, we remember only what we have most recently heard from whoever happened to last have the microphone. The din of opinion often becomes simply noise, and we turn away, no longer listening.

Some issues beg to be thought through. Some issues are so fundamental that we cannot ignore them.

This timely book is an opportunity to pause for a few minutes and reflect on one of the most pressing issues of the day. We have collected into one place the ideas of some of today's most profound religious and spiritual teachers. Each contributor invited to be a part of this unique volume has come to conclusions—not all of them definitive, by any means—grown out of the rich soil of a thoughtful spiritual life.

The questions could hardly be more basic for who we are as a people:

- What are America's responsibilities in the world?
- What should we be doing with our resources, energy, talent, and strength?
- What should we not be doing?

Writing expressly for this volume, sixteen of our most eloquent spiritual teachers—from Protestant, Catholic, Muslim, Jewish, Buddhist, Vedantist, and interfaith traditions—address one overarching question: "What role should America—the only remaining superpower—play in the world?"

Along the way, many other issues are discussed as well, including these:

- How are we like, and different from, superpowers in the past?
- What is the historical background of those ideas that guide us as a people: freedom for all, the balance of individualism and responsibility, inalienable rights, separation of religion and state, and democracy?
- Should spiritual people with spiritual convictions have any influence over national policy?
- What does it mean to be believers and citizens at once?

Specific issues, however, are generally avoided here. Should we deploy troops? How should the United States vote on a particular issue in the United Nations Security Council? Where should we send aid? Larger issues—including historical, moral, and theological ones—are the subjects of these reflections.

Our hope (we the editors and on behalf of our sixteen teachers) is that you will be able to make your own

thoughtful conclusions. Then—and even before then!—
start the discussion in your own local community, church,
synagogue, temple, zendo, retreat center. (See the discussion guide at the back of the book for help on this.)

Part 1 deals with the more basic questions: "How Did
We Get Here? Historical, Political, and Spiritual
Perspectives." How did we become what we undeniably are:
the world's only "superpower," more powerful and more
wealthy than any other nation in history? Roman, Chinese,
Incan, and Spanish empires and other "superpowers" of the
past have not had the reach, influence, resources, and might
that compare with the United States in the twenty-first century. Historians and pundits write books and give speeches
on this subject all the time, but rarely are we given the
opportunity to listen to other perspectives.

Parts 2 and 3 discuss how spiritual people can effect
change around these issues. To use an old phrase, we can
be the change that we seek in the world, and we can do it
through personal action and commitment (part 2) and
through our communities (part 3). Regarding the latter,
Rev. Bill Tully warns us not to prejudge the effectiveness of
communities of faith and spiritual practice:

> Local religious life—by most estimates lived in about
> 350,000 congregations of all kinds—is lively and varied
> and bears little relationship to media preoccupation
> with institutional decline, televangelism, or abusive
> behavior by clergy. Down here, where we live our faith,
> we also think, pray, meditate, and experiment with the
> life-and-death questions.

In every community, Tully writes, there is "leaven in the lump."

Each contributor to *Spiritual Perspectives on America's Role as Superpower* is an American citizen, with the exception of Vietnamese Buddhist teacher Thich Nhat Hanh. As an exile from his homeland for nearly forty years, Thich Nhat Hanh has most often resided in Plum Village, France; but he is really a citizen of the world. His perspective, and his spiritual practice suggestions, are the most unusual contribution to the book.

Despite their American identity, the other contributors offer a great deal of self-criticism in these pages. Rosemary Radford Ruether draws distinct parallels between political and military empires of the past and a clearly emerging American Empire. Rabbi Arthur Waskow uses the analogy of America as "Pharaoh" in the world today. Kabir Helminski uses the metaphor of the global neighborhood to show where he finds us at fault:

> If the world were reduced to the scale of a neighborhood, a third of the neighborhood would be without safe drinking water, sufficient food, and adequate shelter. The United States would be an expensive apartment building with a sophisticated alarm system and armed guards. More and more we disregard the wishes of the neighborhood and resist most attempts to form cooperative organizations to improve our environment or lend a helping hand to our neighbors. We threaten preemptive attacks against neighbors we consider dangerous (or whose real estate we covet?).

Tony Campolo is not the only one to use statistics that paint an unflattering portrait:

> Of the twenty-two industrialized nations of the world, the United States is dead last in per capita giving to the poor peoples of the world. By way of comparison, let me point out that on a per capita basis, for every dollar that America gives to the poor of the world, the people of Norway give seventy.

Each of the contributors seems to believe in the necessity for a frank and honest look at who we are and who we have become.

There is also great optimism here as well. The contributors tend to agree that the United States did not become the most powerful nation in the world by accident. There is something great about the American character and spirit that is not easily found elsewhere. Wayne Teasdale explains:

> It is not an exaggeration to say that in the long, troubled history of this fragile but exquisite planet there has not been a more inventive society than America. It is surely true that there are many societies with equal creativity, i.e., the ancient Greeks, the Arabs during the golden age of Islam, classical China, India, Japan, Germany, France, Spain, and Britain. Then there are the unique approaches to the natural world and culture found in numerous indigenous societies, notably the Australian Aborigines, Native Americans, and the countless tribes of Africa.

Creativity is a universal human attribute, and yet, in the United States this precious trait has received a scope of activity that is virtually unlimited. In this sense, America can be regarded rightly as a multifaceted inventive genius, a practical intelligence that knows no bounds.

Dennis Prager is not just optimistic; he is confident of America's power to do good in the world: "No other country approaches America as a force for good on planet Earth. If a meteor destroyed the United States at this time, the world would be overrun by cruelty."

———

It is for the more than one hundred million Americans who believe that spirituality is essential to life that we created this book. It is for those of us who believe that spirituality is not something quaint, not merely for our personal edification, that we created this book.

Those of us who live with spiritual convictions, or who worship in religious communities, sometimes have the opportunity to hear from the pulpit, from the bima, in the prayer hall, in the zendo, or elsewhere what one spiritual leader believes on these issues. This book is for those of us who want a variety of opinions, for those of us who want to understand the issues more deeply and make up our own minds.

As Americans we have a tradition of working hard to achieve our goals, both national and personal. Once we have determined the direction of our progress and made up our minds, we set out forthrightly on the path to achievement. After reading the words of the teachers in this book, thoughtfully examining our own perspectives, and reaching opinions about the spiritual responsibilities inherent in our individual roles as citizens of the world's only superpower, we must not simply place this book on a shelf and go no further. That's not the American way. We are a people of action—a people of conscience and principle. True to our national heritage, we must stand up and search for others who have come to a similar place of belief. And together we can try to change the world.

Part I

How Did We Get Here?
Historical, Political, and
Spiritual Perspectives

Dual Citizenship
JOHN WILSON

"In a world darkened by sin, both individual and corporate, conflict takes on a tragic dimension. In working toward a good end—or what seems a good end—we often do harm. This is precisely the world as seen in the Bible.

"In World War II, to resist the evil of Nazism, we allied ourselves with the Soviet Union—which had been Hitler's ally until Germany launched a surprise invasion. Together with the Russians, we defeated the Nazis, but our alliance led to the subjugation of millions behind the Iron Curtain in Eastern and Central Europe after the war."

—John Wilson

Editors' note

For those of us within organized religion—of any faith, tradition, or denomination—power is seen through glasses of a particular color. Our traditions answer basic questions that determine how we see reality. Are human beings basically good—or not? What does it mean to be a citizen and a believer at the same time? Is religion relevant to the messy realities of worldly power?

As the founding editor of *Books & Culture,* a journal of Christian opinion not unlike *The New York Review of Books,* John Wilson is both a conservative Christian and an eloquent commentator on the wide range of contemporary culture.

He shows eloquently in this brief essay how working toward a good end can often result in doing harm. Wilson believes that any reflection on America's proper role in the world must first begin with an admission of human sin, ineptitude, and "fallenness," to use the theological term. It is this basic "condition that results not only in tragedy but also in dark absurdity," he reflects.

Wilson is a Christian Realist in the tradition of Reinhold Niebuhr, the early- to mid-twentieth-century American theologian; he explains how we have a responsibility to sometimes accept our responsibility to fight, to make difficult choices in the world of power and politics, without ever rationalizing evil. Referring to recent history, he concludes, "A squad of American soldiers dropped in Afghanistan is at once an emblem of human depravity and of human nobility."

Dual Citizenship
John Wilson

In the controversy over American power and how it should be used, vigorously and often rancorously conducted on talk shows and op-ed pages, in think tanks and policy journals, the matter of a distinctively Christian understanding of the question has hardly been at the forefront, but neither has it been neglected. Indeed, two answers have been heard again and again—two sharply different responses, both of which seem unsatisfactory to me.

The first answer might be called the Way of Renunciation. It is well represented by Daniel Berrigan's just-published book, *Lamentations: From New York to Kabul and Beyond,* in which Berrigan reflects on September 11 and its aftermath in the light of the Lamentations of the prophet Jeremiah. Castigating President Bush and his "war on terror," equally critical of the church for its complicity with the "warmaking state," Berrigan calls for "another way," renouncing "retaliation and revenge" and instead embarking on a national confession of sin.

Many Christian thinkers have agreed. In the final week of the year, I was in Atlanta for an InterVarsity Grad and Faculty Ministries conference, "Following Christ 2002." During that week, the murder of three Christian missionaries in Yemen was reported, with a statement from the U.S. government saying that those responsible would be "hunted down." It should not be so, said my friend, the systematic theologian Miroslav Volf, one of the plenary speakers at the conference. Hunting down the murderers is *not* what the martyred missionaries themselves would have wanted: such a response violates the meaning of their witness.

In general, those who argue for the Way of Renunciation believe that the Christian perspective on America's role as a superpower is painfully clear. Renounce war; renounce power. Resist the evil machinations of the state; repent for the weakness of the church, for the failure of Christians to take up the cross. What we are called to do may indeed be difficult, but it is straightforward, without ambiguity.

On the other hand, there is the Way of Realpolitik. It is well represented by Robert Kaplan's book *Warrior Politics: Why Leadership Demands a Pagan Ethos*. From this point of view, the radical meditations of a Daniel Berrigan are so peripheral as to be beneath notice. What is dangerous, say the practitioners of Realpolitik, is a more diffuse Christian sentimentality about America and its role in the world. Such sentimentality makes it difficult for America to acknowledge the reality of its own power and to exercise it effectively. Ruthlessness, stealth, and cunning are the attributes we need in our leaders, not "Christian" virtues.

Kaplan concedes that some Christians, from Augustine to Reinhold Niebuhr, have been political realists, but he misconstrues their engagement with the world: "What all these men were groping for, it seems, was a way to use pagan, public morality to advance—albeit indirectly— private, Judeo-Christian morality." Here, in Kaplan's unwit- ting condescension, his genial contempt for religion is all too apparent.

Indeed, in one important respect, the Way of Renunciation and the Way of Realpolitik are in fundamental agreement: Christianity is irrelevant to the messy realities of power. But is this really true?

James Q. Wilson and Edward Banfield began their classic study *City Politics* (1966) with the observation that "politics arises out of conflicts, and it consists of the activities—for example, reasonable discussion, impassioned oratory, balloting, and street fighting—by which conflict is carried on." This is no less true of international politics than of city politics. In a world darkened by sin, both individual and corporate, conflict takes on a tragic dimension. In working toward a good end—or what seems a good end—we often do harm. This is precisely the world as seen in the Bible.

In World War II, to resist the evil of Nazism, we allied ourselves with the Soviet Union—which had been Hitler's ally until Germany launched a surprise invasion. Together with the Russians, we defeated the Nazis, but our alliance led to the subjugation of millions behind the Iron Curtain in Eastern and Central Europe after the war.

Far from being doomed to sentimentality, a Christian understanding of politics—and hence a Christian perspective on America's role as a superpower—must begin with our fallenness, a condition that results not only in tragedy but also in dark absurdity. And yet we are also human beings created in the very image of God, a little lower than the angels. A squad of American soldiers dropped in Afghanistan is at once an emblem of human depravity and of human nobility.

To be Christian Realists—to borrow Niebuhr's term—we need to learn both from the Way of Renunciation and from the Way of Realpolitik. If we pride ourselves on our realism, we may soon end up rationalizing evil. Such was the case with United States policy in Central America under the Reagan administration. Beware the siren song of Realpolitik, as crooned by Henry Kissinger! But if we pride ourselves on our radical Christian stance, we may abdicate our responsibility to fight the good fight, to make tough choices in a messy, ever-shifting political landscape.

Here, and here, and there, with Christ in us, we dwell in the kingdom of God, awaiting its fulfillment. This knowledge will not help us to decide whether the United States should invade Iraq, or how best to go about responding to the AIDS crisis in Africa, but it should establish the framework in which—with all due humility—we try to answer such questions, as dual citizens of the City of God and the City of Man.

From Nationalism to Patriotism: Reclaiming the American Creed

REV. FORREST CHURCH

"The spiritual response to America's global status springs from deep moral conviction. Initially the hope was that America—by becoming a superpower—would save the world. Today the fear is that America—having become a superpower—will destroy it. Both fear and hope are exaggerated, but there is ample reason for each. On one hand, as long as American Empire follows the pulse of American nationalism ('America first'), one can legitimately fear that others in the world will ultimately suffer from American hegemony. On the other, to whatever extent our policies are inspired by the patriotic ideals of the nation's founders ('liberty and justice for all'), one can dare to hope that America will yet fulfill a noble global mission."

—Rev. Forrest Church

Editors' note

Did America's first adventures as a superpower at the end of the nineteenth century have an evangelical subtext from the very beginning? Rev. Forrest Church makes a strong case for the historical export of Protestant Christianity and American democracy in the same package—the Bible leading the gun, so to speak. In a fascinating survey of America's involvement beyond its own borders, Church makes it clear that the establishment of an ecumenically sponsored missionary movement went hand in glove with the extension of American military might. And yet the compelling question he asks is, What has this led us to?

American patriotism, says Church, demands a high level of moral engagement. If all people are created equal and endowed by their Creator with inalienable rights, "all people" represents more than merely the people of the United States. And if this is true, then we are called to a higher mandate than the mere extension of American power. We may not isolate ourselves as the world's superpower in the name of American nationalism. Our destiny is meant to be fulfilled—or betrayed—on the international stage.

From Nationalism to Patriotism:
Reclaiming the American Creed
Rev. Forrest Church

I n the 1890s, when the national ship of state lifted anchor to claim islands in two of the seven seas, the religious response at home to America's emergence abroad as a budding superpower might best be described as a rousing "Amen." Today, little more than a century later, an ecumenical coalition as broad as that which earlier had blessed such forays greets America's latest international adventures with wholesale condemnation. In both instances, the spiritual response to America's global status springs from deep moral conviction. Initially the hope was that America—by becoming a superpower—would save the world. Today the fear is that America—having become a superpower—will destroy it.

Both fear and hope are exaggerated, but there is ample reason for each. On one hand, as long as American Empire follows the pulse of American nationalism ("America first"), one can legitimately fear that others in the world will ultimately suffer from American hegemony. On the other, to whatever extent our policies are inspired by the patriotic ideals of the nation's founders ("liberty and justice for all"), one can dare to hope that America will yet fulfill a noble global mission.

The concept of American Empire first emerged in the 1890s. Manifest Destiny was its watchword, its staging areas mostly islands and archipelagos from Cuba to the Philippines. Though its architects, principal among them Theodore Roosevelt, John Hay, Henry Cabot Lodge, and

Albert Beveridge, were not conspicuously pious men, American Empire had an evangelical subtext from the very beginning. American internationalism commenced, in fact, with American Missions. The gun came quickly to hand, but Manifest Destiny led with a prayer book. A band of Christian evangelists set the tempo for America's march into world history.

Josiah Strong, a young Congregationalist pastor and evangelist, wrote the first manifesto for American internationalism in 1885. An instant best seller, *Our Country: Its Possible Future and Its Present Crisis* set the moral tone for American expansion. Its popularity led to Strong's appointment as general secretary of the Evangelical Alliance, a leading vehicle for social reform and Christian mission. Strong believed that American Protestantism—ecumenical in spirit and practice—was the perfect catalyst to redeem a divided world. Dedicated to the social gospel, he called for an international crusade to nurture the spirit of liberty and equality, foster peace, and enhance security—all in preparation for the establishment of God's kingdom. Wedding biblical religion to republican faith, Strong rallied his countrymen to accomplish "the evangelization of the world."

Both as an evangelical Christian and as a social liberal, Strong viewed American expansionism as a spiritual, not a business, imperative. He celebrated the extension of free markets as conduits for Christian and American ideals. Yet, as subsequent American internationalists have also often been, Strong was remarkably parochial. To him, American empire would signal the triumph of Anglo-Saxon values and culture. The net result was white-bread

Christian American jingoism. "We are the chosen people," Strong proclaimed. "We cannot afford to wait. The plans of God will not wait. Those plans seem to have brought us to one of the closing stages in the world's career, in which we can no long drift with safety to our destiny."

Strong's call was answered in two ways: first by the establishment and rapid growth of an ecumenically sponsored missionary movement, and second by the extension of military might beyond the nation's borders. Protestant Christianity and American democracy were exported in the same package. The union of faith and freedom we had established at home would be promulgated abroad. To accomplish this, if need be, American values would be supported by American arms.

In retrospect, America's first adventures as a superpower were more than a little ham-fisted. To begin with, the level of ignorance in the White House and State Department about this world we were setting out to redeem was nothing short of remarkable. President William McKinley's only stated justification for going to war with Spain in 1898 was "to Christianize the Philippines," which happened already to be Christian. Nonetheless, by the end of World War I, President Woodrow Wilson had codified an explicit religious mission for the nation's international agenda. "I, for one, believe more profoundly than in anything else human in the destiny of the United States," he said. "I believe that she has a spiritual energy in her which no other nation can contribute to the liberation of mankind."

Sailing across the Atlantic to take part in the peace conference after the war, Wilson was even more explicit about our newfound mission as a superpower. "We are to be an instrument in the hands of God to see that liberty is made secure for mankind," he said. In this conviction, Wilson was not alone. Many Christian ministers—including Lyman Abbott, known for his commitment to the social gospel—viewed what turned out to be World War I as a "twentieth-century crusade." That any religious meaning could be wrung out of that conflict demonstrates how quick Americans are to invest their national endeavors with religious portent.

We can learn a lesson from the early collusion of religion with the nation's international agenda. As American Empire extended its circle of influence, religious leaders, at the risk of their own integrity, were increasingly tempted to subjugate their theological principles to the interests of American foreign policy. Shortly after World War I ended, to attract converts the Christian Scientists ran a full-page ad in the *New York Times* proclaiming the credo of their founder, Mary Baker Eddy. The ordering of her beliefs is telling: "I believe strictly in the Monroe Doctrine, in our Constitution, and in the laws of God."

Americans have long rationalized national and international policies by religious and moral argument. Whenever they do so, as both Strong's and Wilson's rhetoric suggests, one longs for a dose of Abraham Lincoln's dour theological realism. Lincoln never accepted the proposition that God was on our side. He strove instead to ensure that our actions would place us on the side of God.

Nonetheless, that American policy should be charged with religious mission does not, in and of itself, constitute a betrayal of either national or religious ideals. Implicit in the overarching faith sponsored by pluralistic democracy is an evangelical charge. If all people are created equal and are endowed by their Creator with certain inalienable rights, "all people" represents more than merely the people of the United States. American patriotism demands a high level of moral engagement. In this respect, American isolationism is an oxymoron. Today, as the world's only superpower, how we express our ideals internationally is of utmost importance to people throughout the world.

Conversely, American nationalism is insufficient to the moral requirements inherent to our fulfillment of this solemn responsibility. There is nothing unique about American nationalism. As with every expression of nationalism, it is grounded in the first law of nature—self-protection. Other countries may benefit from a superpower's nationalistic policies, but their own interests remain secondary. Even the most enlightened nationalism, therefore, breeds resentment. President George W. Bush may be absolutely right about the pressing need to disarm Saddam Hussein, but by offering this as an American imperative he must not be surprised that the world feels bullied.

Unlike American nationalism, American patriotism is unique. The United States of America is "the only nation in the world that is founded on a creed ... set forth with almost dogmatic and even theological lucidity in the Declaration of Independence," wrote a British observer, G. K. Chesterton. Expanding the compass of natural law, the founders extended the people's inalienable rights from safety alone to liberty and equality. As summed up in the nation's motto, *E pluribus unum* ("out of many, one"), this creed is universal, not parochial. It does not read "All Americans are created equal." To the extent that the United States betrays its own ideals, American patriotism holds the nation under judgment.

It has done so from the beginning. When established as national writ, "All men are created equal" excluded both women and slaves. The first feminist manifesto (written by Elizabeth Cady Stanton in 1848) invoked the Declaration of Independence to point out the gap between deed and creed. In condemning the curse of slavery, Frederick Douglass and Abraham Lincoln did the same. Expressing his dream, the Rev. Dr. Martin Luther King Jr. looked "forward to the day that this nation will rise up and live out the true meaning of its creed." From the outset of our history, American patriots have challenged the nation to tune its actions to the key of its ideals. In his study of American racism, the Swedish economist Gunnar Myrdal described American history as "the gradual realization of the American Creed."

Today we fulfill or betray our national destiny most dramatically on the international stage. Abraham Lincoln recognized that the Declaration of Independence "gave liberty not alone to the people of this country, but hope to all the world, for all future time." On a shrinking globe where discrete backyards no longer exist, the American ideal of *E pluribus unum* has become an international mandate. Our greatest leaders recognized this half a century ago. President Franklin Delano Roosevelt applied his "Four Freedoms" (freedom from want and fear, freedom of faith and speech) "everywhere in the world." As chair of the Human Rights Commission of a new United Nations, Eleanor Roosevelt coauthored the Universal Declaration of Human Rights, a global restatement of America's principles of liberty and justice for all. As adopted by the United Nations General Assembly on December 10, 1948, the Universal Declaration of Human Rights explicitly echoes Jefferson's words in the Declaration of Independence. All people are equally "endowed with reason and conscience." The preamble declares that "recognition of the inherent dignity and of the equal and inalienable rights of all members of the human family is the foundation of freedom, justice, and peace in the world." By affirming and expanding the founders' vision of "out of many, one," the United Nations is itself the greatest monument to American patriotism.

Terrorism is not an American problem; it is a world problem. The battle against terror—not a clash of civilizations but a clash between civilization and anarchy—demands an international front, not a self-appointed savior. American arrogance can only fan the flames American policy is designed to extinguish. One sets a backfire to control a burning forest only when the winds are favorable. Otherwise the backfire spreads the very flames that it was intended to quench. Beyond going against the logic of enlightened self-interest, policies that impose an American agenda (simply because American power is sufficient to implement American desire) take a high spiritual toll on the nation itself. From a religious perspective, arrogance expresses pride, and pride is rightly considered the number one sin.

The impulse of American nationalism isolates the United States and turns others against us. It also rescinds the nation's greatest gift. As the world's leaders struggle to act together—whether to slow global warming, ban land mines, combat racism, or create an International Criminal Court—the president of the United States is conspicuously absent. We have isolated ourselves from the very councils we are charged, by both power and principle, to lead. At a time when *E pluribus unum*—however idealistic, however difficult to accomplish—is becoming the world's motto, the United States, whose founders gave this vision as a gift to the world, increasingly stands alone.

What a lost opportunity this represents. Recognizing their own tears in American eyes, people throughout the world expressed unprecedented sympathy for our nation in the wake of September 11. President Jacques Chirac of France proclaimed, "We are all Americans now." Today even America is divided against itself. To have squandered both the world's affection and the united spirit of our citizenry in little more than a year represents a tragic triumph of American nationalism over American patriotism.

During the first chapter of American Empire, the mission embarked on by Josiah Strong and other Christian missionaries was well intentioned: to ameliorate social conditions throughout the world and to spread the American faith in liberty and justice for all. Our leaders make similar moral claims today. America can and must witness to the higher principles on which this nation is founded. Yet, so long as American superpower is indistinguishable from American nationalism writ large, we betray the very moral principles to which we give self-serving lip service. By so doing, we can only add to the problems we are trying to solve.

The most recent chapter of our history is not alone in reminding us that nationalism can be as blind as love, for it is a form of love. Searching through my grandparents' attic when I was a boy, I found a handsome wooden plaque picturing a soldier in a broad-brimmed American World War I helmet and embossed in burnished copper with the words "My country, right or wrong." In coining this phrase in 1816, Stephan Decatur (though expressing a preference that his country would turn out to be right, not wrong), proposed the ultimate toast to nationalism. Since responsible power calls itself under judgment, American patriotism refutes this sentiment by emending it more pointedly. Speaking against the extension of Manifest Destiny into the Philippines in 1899, Senator Carl Schurz of Missouri said, "Our country, right or wrong. When right, to be kept right; when wrong, to be put right."

The United States is built on a foundation of belief, not on a foundation of skepticism. By our actions, not our words, this foundation of belief is either justified or betrayed. "An almost chosen people" (in Lincoln's words), we demonstrate our greatness not by force of might or by virtue of our economic dominance but through rigorous moral endeavor, ever striving to remake ourselves in the image of our ideals. Patriotic fidelity to the nation's creed remains challenging, but it invests the nation with spiritual purpose and—if we honor its precepts—a moral destiny. American nationalism betrays that destiny. What we need today are a few more patriots.

Spiritual Reflections on America in a Global Neighborhood

KABIR HELMINSKI

"We forget that during the twentieth century the great majority of intellectuals in Muslim lands, despite the injustices of colonialism, were enamored of America and the West. We have squandered that goodwill, alienating the majority and sprinkling gasoline on the dying embers of Islamic fundamentalism, which had more or less shown itself to be bereft of any practical solutions to the problems of Muslim peoples. I repeat: Islamic fundamentalism was a lost cause until we gave it new life through our own ill-considered policies and self-righteous rhetoric."

—Kabir Helminski

Editors' note

As a Shaikh of the Sufi Mevlevi Order (the order of the poet Rumi) Kabir Helminski has a sensitive ear and eye for the effects of American influence in Muslim countries. We have squandered the goodwill that many Muslim leaders and intellectuals once had for us, earlier in the twentieth century, he says, "sprinkling gasoline on the dying embers of Islamic fundamentalism, which had more or less shown itself to be bereft of any practical solutions to the problems of Muslim peoples."

Helminski believes that what makes Americans truly American is what can also lead the way back to our playing a more positive role in world affairs. He focuses our attention on what the Qur'an refers to as "those who are faithful and accomplish the good." But it is not in organized religion that he thinks we will find the answers. There is a distinctively American ethos and character, with deep roots in ideas and practices, that can show us how to be faithful and accomplish the good once again.

The "American character" features a strong sense of the moral authority of the individual conscience, the power of spiritual individualism, and a useful pragmatism. It is these basic instincts—and a renewed commitment to the constitutional rights to life, liberty, and the pursuit of happiness—Helminski believes, that can still allow America to fulfill its destiny in the world.

Spiritual Reflections on America in a Global Neighborhood
Kabir Helminski

What is this phenomenon we call "America"? In recent centuries it has occupied a prominent place in the imagination of humanity as a social experiment involving certain unique features: government by and for the people, yet with limited powers; ethnic and religious diversity; a geography endowed with immense resources and relative security.

If we look to our roots, we see that America began in rebellion against monarchism and empire. The idea of a sovereign republic proposes to guarantee the rights of individual human beings, not as mere economic entities but as souls having the right to life, liberty, and the pursuit of happiness—significantly because the founding fathers debated and rejected another phrase in its place: the protection of property.

The idea of the republic is not only to guarantee the rights of the individual but to guarantee the common good as well, for if the rights of certain individuals are more guaranteed than those of others, the rights of all are compromised. American values are between these two poles: that of the individual good and that of the common good.

A notion commonly expressed by the Christian right is that American democracy and evangelical Christianity are somehow uniquely partners in this great experiment. This belief belies the fact that key formulators of our country's ideals and system of government were not conventional

Christians but deists or Freemasons: Franklin, Washington, Jefferson, and approximately half of the signers of the Declaration of Independence and the Constitution were clearly in this category. America at the time of its founding was a unique experiment in religious pluralism and secularism, a unique challenge to the ideas of ecclesiastical power, inherited authority, and imperialism.

Half a century after the founding of the republic, a philosophical and spiritual revival in New England expressed certain ideals that would further shape the American character: a preoccupation with the moral authority of the individual conscience. Emerson was its finest representative: "I like the silent church before the service begins, better than any preaching." In other words, he respected the collective effort to draw near to the divine presence but saw little value in the retail moralizing offered by preachers. As he said elsewhere: "Each cause—say abolitionism, temperance, say Calvinism or Unitarianism—becomes speedily a little shop, where the article, let it at first have been ever so subtle and ethereal, is now made up into portable and convenient cakes, and retailed in small quantities to suit purchasers."[1]

Emerson represented a romantic notion of the ideal of American character, the idealist and independent thinker standing apart from the herd. In a letter to Oliver Wendell Holmes, Emerson wrote: "A scholar need not be so cynical to feel that the vast multitude are almost on all fours, that the rich always vote after their fears that cities churches colleges all go for the quadruped interest, and it is against this coalition that the pathetically small minority of disengaged and thinking men stand for the ideal right, for man as he should be, and (what is essential in any sane maintenance of his own right) for the right of every other as his own."[2]

Emerson's spiritual individualism represents one pole of the American character. To keep a balanced view, there is another mentality that sees Christian faith not as a mere joining of the herd, not as an arbitrary revelation triumphing over reason, but as the fulfillment of reason. Coleridge was an important spokesman for this point of view, and he influenced many thinkers in America, especially through his work *Aids to Reflection*, published in 1829. He represents in many ways the best of the Christian temperament. Human beings are not a blank slate ready to have anything written upon them, as Locke proposed, but we are each bearers of a divine imprint. This is identical to the Islamic notion that human beings were created from "a beautiful archetype," that faith is somehow inscribed on our hearts.

From this point of view, faith is the perfection of human reason. There are not two sets of laws, one based on religion and revelation, another based on science and philosophy, which has been very much a tradition of Continental Europe, especially those countries dominated by Catholicism. This middle way, more typical of the English mentality, which came to be inherited by America, is that faith and reason can be reconciled, that faith is the empirical experience of contemplating our own souls and discovering there an objective truth of the heart. This, too, is consonant with the fundamental Quranic notion that the physical world reveals the divine qualities to those who reflect. From this point of view, science cannot be a threat to faith.

Furthermore, Emerson's radical individualism—the paramount importance of individual, self-realized conscience—must, however, be tempered by the idea of community, because the human being can discover its true self only in relation to a wider community. It is a reciprocal relationship. In other words, we discover who we are as individuals in relationship to a community. This applies to nations just as it applies to individuals.

Another major feature of the American character is pragmatism: a concern not with an ideal truth but with the usefulness and practicality of any idea. For the pragmatist, something is true if it works. The value of ideas is judged not by the logic of some immutable eternal ideal but by the quality of life such an idea engenders. Actually, this is also in accord with the Quranic notion that faith is linked to righteous action. The Qur'an refers countless times to *those who are faithful and accomplish the good.* The fundamental idea of faith in God has survived and endured because it has supported and refined human life. This faith, however, ought to be distinguished from the conformist mentality of organized religion. "Religion" is always used as the justification for some of the worst evils men can conceive of. Oliver Wendell Holmes, following in the footsteps of Emerson's thought, took aim at the religious conformism that condoned the institution of slavery as if one group of men could "own other men by God's Law."

America has this tradition of critical conscience, and it also has its mainstream of a conventional, compromised amorality supported by high notions of moral rectitude. In our own time America seems to be moving toward a concept of civilization that justifies the use of overwhelming power against those who, we imagine, do not share our idea of civilization. It is a concept of civilization that forfeits the moral high ground even while it claims to establish it.

It would be interesting to return to Emerson to consider his reflections on the most notorious figure of the eighteenth century, Napoleon Bonaparte, whom Emerson profiled in his book *Representative Men*. For him Napoleon captured the fascination of Everyman because he was Everyman writ large: "The idol of common men because he had in transcendent degrees the qualities and powers of common men." Napoleon subordinated all values—spiritual, cultural, and moral—to his own egoistic, materialistic ends; he was a thoroughly modern hero of the commercial class, devoid of idealism but using idealism for his own purposes. Napoleon's glory "passed away like the smoke of his artillery, and left no trace. He left France smaller, poorer, feebler than he found it."[3]

It is a grace that the United States of America has avoided giving rise to a Napoleon in its two-hundred-fifty-year history. But that may be about to change if we are entering our own undisguised imperial phase.

Our founding fathers were not the first to recognize the dangers of the incremental abuse of power and to recommend the fastidious observance of fairness. Take this tale told by the Persian Sufi poet Sadi in the thirteenth century:

> While out on a hunt one day with the King, they were about to cook some kebabs when it was learned that the party had no salt. The monarch sent a servant to a nearby village to fetch some salt, instructing him,

however, to pay a fair price for the salt. Some asked the King what harm could come from just asking for the salt, rather than buying it. The King responded that it was necessary to pay for the salt so that the exaction of salt by the King not turn into a custom that would one day ruin the village. "Oppression has been brought into the world from such small beginnings, which every newcomer has increased, until it has reached the present degree of enormity. If a King were to eat a single apple from an orchard, eventually his ministers would appropriate the whole orchard, and if the King were to borrow five eggs, soon a thousand chickens would be barbecued. Long after the tyrant has passed from the world, the curses of mankind would still be heard."

As America, now the only superpower, appears to be embarking on its own unabashedly imperial phase, it appears to be incrementally betraying the values upon which it was founded. Amid a flurry of self-righteous rhetoric about "protecting our way of life," it is shocking how much of our freedom, economic well-being, and environment are under assault. One needs to propose no hidden conspiracy other than the inevitable coercion ensuing from the accumulation of wealth and power in the hands of the few, arrogantly and ignorantly obsessed with their own short-term advantage. It is a failure of justice and love.

Pragmatically speaking, the selfish human ego, and any nation that attempts to live according to egoistic values, does not create civilization but only contributes to civilization's decadence. The best chance for civilization lies with the idea that there is a correspondence between the human realm and the spiritual realm and that in this world we should strive to bring the two together. Another, more Christian way of expressing this is that we are made in the "image of God." Egoism leads sooner or later to disintegration. Spiritual values, not mere self-righteous lip service to them, lead to tolerance, patience, forgiveness, cooperation, generosity, and, yes, love.

In these days when there is talk of a clash of civilizations, when a new enemy has been summoned like a genie out of a bottle, we forget that during the twentieth century the great majority of intellectuals in Muslim lands, despite the injustices of colonialism, were enamored of America and the West. We have squandered that goodwill, alienating the majority and sprinkling gasoline on the dying embers of Islamic fundamentalism, which had more or less shown itself to be bereft of any practical solutions to the problems of Muslim peoples. I repeat: Islamic fundamentalism was a lost cause until we gave it new life through our own ill-considered policies and self-righteous rhetoric. In our blind support of the worst elements of Zionism (at the expense of the overall well-being and security of Israel), in our cynical use of power in Central Asia (aimed at control of its immense resources), in our unholy alliances with Middle Eastern dictators (attempting to guarantee a comfortable status quo for our own corporations), we have lost the trust and respect of the Muslim world.

We are losing the respect and trust of Europe and the rest of the world as well. Our abandonment of treaty obligations, our disregard of international law, our undermin-

ing of institutions for international justice, our unwilling-
ness to support an international court of criminal justice,
our noncooperation with international environmental ini-
tiatives, and our blocking of programs to meet the basic
needs of the world's poorest peoples have only underlined
the hypocrisy of our rhetoric.

If the world were reduced to the scale of a neighborhood, a third of the neighborhood would be without safe
drinking water, sufficient food, and adequate shelter. The
United States would be an expensive apartment building
with a sophisticated alarm system and armed guards. More
and more we disregard the wishes of the neighborhood and
resist most attempts to form cooperative organizations to
improve our environment or lend a helping hand to our
neighbors. We threaten preemptive attacks against neighbors we consider dangerous (or whose real estate we
covet?).

At the same time we are in denial about the great contradictions within our own society. We needn't describe in
detail the victimization, substance abuse, and mindless
entertainments going on there as the majority of its resi-
dents rest assured of their moral superiority and the divine
sanction of their economic privilege. Meanwhile we live in
a state of fear, bewildered as to why our neighbors do not
appreciate us, asserting that they hate us for our "love of
freedom."

In an interview I recently heard, an Iraqi woman on
the street in Baghdad said, "Americans are a very aggressive people. They need to realize that they are not better
than other people; they are just the same as the rest of the

world, no better." In other words, it appears to many in the world that America is acting like the immature bully of the planet.

Regarding the current bogus "clash of civilizations," we must understand that while Islamic extremism is a real if overrated danger, traditional Islam, quite to the contrary, has offered a truly humane and multicultural perspective. The various religious communities of Jerusalem prospered and were protected during thirteen centuries of mostly Islamic rule. Islamic Spain was the crucible in which Judaism attained some of its highest intellectual and spiritual achievements. The Ottoman Empire for five centuries welcomed minorities, including Slavs, Greeks, Armenians, Arab Christians, and the Jews expelled from Spain, into a productive multicultural society. We are making a big mistake if we lose the goodwill of this potential ally in the struggle to preserve our own humanity.

In addition, Islamic culture has a great deal to teach us regarding the dangers of usury and speculative finance, as well as the right use of capital for human purposes. Furthermore, as most visitors to Muslim countries would testify, Islamic culture can teach us much about the virtues of personal humility, civility, and hospitality, even as our own Western culture seems to be sinking into a depersonalization verging on barbarism.

I still have not lost hope that America has a destiny to fulfill. If we can regain our alignment with our own Constitution and Bill of Rights, if we support in the world what we would like to have for ourselves—namely, the right to life, liberty, and the pursuit of happiness; and government of the people, by the people, and for the people—we may be able to fulfill that destiny. If we can keep alive that "self-reliance" that Emerson proposed, in which the "self" is something much greater than the individual ego, we might find our way. America is not a Christian nation, as some propose, but we could be a God-conscious nation, as our founders hoped.

Inevitably there will be clashes when we are faced with the difficult equations that political reality presents us, but we will have a better chance of solving these difficult equations if we rise above the motivations of greed and fear, if we commit ourselves to being generous and just, if we can humble ourselves enough to be not a military but a moral superpower. The central political questions facing us today might be these: What prevents us from acting with more generosity and compassion? Why don't we have leaders that point the way toward a more idealistic and virtuous America? Given our current preeminence, why do we continue to misuse our vast power, and where is it leading us?

---

1. "The Transcendentalist" (1842), in *Essays*, edited by Alfred R. Ferguson and Jean F. Carr (Cambridge: Harvard University Press, 1983).

2. *The Letters of Ralph Waldo Emerson*, edited by R. L. Rusk (New York: Columbia University Press, 1939), 5:17.

3. *Representative Men*, in *Collected Words of Emerson*, 4:224.

Called to the Task of Peacemaker

REV. DR. JOAN BROWN CAMPBELL

"We think of ourselves as a nation of faithful people responsive to God's will and God's way. If this is true, then we would be clear that our power and abundance came to us not by our own work and will but was given to us by our Creator to be carefully tended and fully shared. The attitude held by some people that abundance is a reward for right behavior has played out in exploitation and even slavery. The dream set forth in our founding documents calls for equality, and from that dream flows our moral authority."

—Rev. Dr. Joan Brown Campbell

Editors' note

A life spent as a leader in the ecumenical interfaith movement and her personal participation in some of the great historic events of the past century have allowed Rev. Dr. Joan Brown Campbell to take a truly global view of America's responsibilities as the last remaining superpower. From her vantage point as an ordained minister in two Christian denominations, she summarizes the American moral imperative established in our Constitution and demands that we step up to the responsibilities of fulfilling the dream of equality for all citizens of the world without flinching.

Rev. Dr. Campbell gets right to the heart of the matter in her contribution to this volume: In a democracy, citizens must act on their conscience. When she mentions the work of Dr. Martin Luther King Jr., she writes as someone who brought him to her own congregation when it was the first white church in Cleveland to receive him. When she urges Americans to take on the role of peacemaker for the world, it is with the experience gained during her years leading the National Council of Churches and the United States office of the World Council of Churches.

And she asks, What must we relinquish if we are called to be the peacemaker in our troubled world? Will we have the strength to serve in a humble spirit?

Called to the Task of Peacemaker
Rev. Dr. Joan Brown Campbell

The United States, by all accounts, is the only remaining superpower in the world. For many, this unarguable fact is a matter of pride. The leaders of this nation are the most influential decision makers in the world. Their decisions have life-and-death implications for people all around the globe. This is an awesome responsibility and should, in fact, be a sobering encounter with the possibilities and choices that must be faced every single day.

The biblical command, in the face of such power, is quite clear. Scripture tells us that "unto whom much is given, much is required." The assumption is that abundance carries a moral imperative. We are a nation blessed not only with power but also with wealth. We have the capacity to care for our own citizens and also to export that ethic to the entire planet. Our nation has the resources to feed, clothe, house, and heal its people, and it has the moral responsibility to do just that. Failure to share the God-given abundance that has blessed this land and its people reveals a spiritual weakness.

We think of ourselves as a nation of faithful people responsive to God's will and God's way. If this is true, then we would be clear that our power and abundance came to us not by our own work and will but was given to us by our Creator to be carefully tended and fully shared. The attitude held by some people that abundance is a reward for right behavior has played out in exploitation and even slavery. The dream set forth in our founding documents calls for equality, and from that dream flows our moral authority. The words of these documents have such enduring power that they have been copied in constitutions around the world. The right to life, liberty, and the pursuit of happiness is a noble goal.

It was this vision of an America that is just and accords dignity to all its citizens and others throughout the world that captured Rev. Martin Luther King Jr. He dared to assume that all Americans wished to live this dream. In words of exquisite eloquence, he set this dream before the American people, and the nation was confronted with the disparity between our national vision and the stark reality of lives destroyed by bigotry and prejudice. Martin Luther King Jr. spoke truth to power, and the nation changed, and it cost him his life.

Today, our failure to see our own weaknesses becomes incandescently clear as our brash behavior calls the world to live in the way we see as best. We have taken on the role of policeman and judge to the world. Yet, our spiritual and moral weakness renders us not only ineffective but also spiritually impoverished. We call the whole world to disarm as we spend billions of dollars preparing for war and amassing our armed forces in preparation to fight. The moral authority that is embedded in our national vision carries no weight in the face of our behavior.

If we want the world to disarm, then would it not be prudent for us to go to the United Nations and lay out our own nuclear capacity? Would not our moral authority be enhanced if we said to the world that we harbor weapons of mass destruction? If we expect the world to trust us, knowing that we have weapons of mass destruction, if we want the world to believe that these weapons exist purely to prove our dominance, then we must set forth as peacemakers and, by example, lay a path that leads to peace. Preparation for war is an act of violence, and violence is always a spiritual failure. Only as we show ourselves willing to live nonviolently will we be able to call the world to trust us as peacemakers.

In the face of our power, humility is our only spiritual weapon. Much is required of us. Perhaps we are required to risk losing our power in order to gain life for the world—which is, after all, God's gift to all of God's children. It seems quite unlikely that we might willingly give up our privileged status, but that may just be what is required of us. The world is on the brink of war, and maybe even annihilation. We are being called to the task of peacemaker.

Superpower versus Spiritual Power— Choosing Wisely

MATTHEW FOX

"The historical Jesus made an alternative to the superpower of his day the very cornerstone of his teaching. For every time he spoke of the 'kingdom of God' (which he did often), he was tweaking the Romans for running their empire so cruelly. Jesus offered an alternative to the power thinking of his day that would imitate creation and would be based on justice and compassion for the oppressed."

—Matthew Fox

Editors' note

Matthew Fox surprises us when he begins, "The spiritual is about power, about using power well and rightly." But he is right. There are healthy forms of spirituality and not-so-healthy ones, too.

Fox argues that we who are spiritually inclined should know better than to allow unfettered power that is not for the greater good. He identifies a great deal of inappropriateness in the use of American power.

In order to find the truth in these matters, Fox believes in recovering the important skill of self-criticism—a skill too often set aside in America during critical times. "A superpower must be super in its capacity to criticize itself and learn and speak the truth. How well are we doing?" Fox worries about our seeming inability to look critically at ourselves: on the level of personal responsibility and as a nation. Power without the exercise of this skill is most likely not "super" at all.

"To take on the mantle of 'superpower' is to presume that we have something colossal to share with the rest of the world," Fox reflects. But, after considering the United States commitment—or relative lack of commitment—to end hunger within its borders, wipe out corporate corruption, protect natural resources, achieve equity in the workplace, and more—he concludes: Not so fast.

Superpower versus Spiritual Power—
Choosing Wisely
Matthew Fox

The spiritual is about power, about using power well and rightly. Sacred objects are called power objects. And a holy person is said to possess healing powers and power within. Healthy spirituality empowers people, especially the poor and oppressed.

Yet, the word "power" remains an ambiguous concept. What is power for? What are the limits of power? Why seek power?

Just what is a superpower? Is "superpower" related to "superman" and "supermouse"? Is it about myths of superiority and lording over others? About saving the world, as in a messiah complex? About "surpassing all others"? And who anoints one a "superpower"? Power can be addictive. Is superpower super addictive?

How closely allied to imperialism is a superpower? When you add the word "empire" to "superpower," things really get scary. There are government employees today in the Bush administration who have been publishing articles for years on the need for Americans to stand up for an American empire.

All this makes me blush with embarrassment. Did our founding fathers seek that we become the new empire—after so many had fled the empires of England, Spain, Portugal, and France? Why should we seek to be an empire or a superpower—whatever that means. I think it means that everyone should imitate our lifestyle and our version of culture. But I, as an American citizen who still votes (a shrinking minority in our country), have never seen on a ballot the invitation to decide on whether we want to be (1) a superpower and (2) an empire or (3) just right all the time and smarter than every other country because our army is the biggest and mightiest. (So too are our prison population and our homelessness and our gap between obscenely rich and obscenely poor and the number of persons we put to death in the name of capital punishment.)

In the Hebrew Bible, one superpower is Egypt, and the Pharaoh is its arm. Neither comes off looking very good in the eyes of God, whose power alone we are instructed to admire. Anything else is called a major sin, idolatry, or the worshiping of false power objects.

Superpowers are addressed in the Christian Bible as well. The historical Jesus made an alternative to the super-power of his day the very cornerstone of his teaching. For every time he spoke of the "kingdom of God" (which he did often), he was tweaking the Romans for running their empire so cruelly. Jesus offered an alternative to the power thinking of his day that would imitate creation and would be based on justice and compassion for the oppressed.

In the last book of the Christian Bible, the issue of empire and superpower is discussed with much vehe-mence. In the book of Revelation we read all about the superpower of that day. The Roman Empire was doing all it could to wipe out the upstart Christians, including—but not limited to—throwing them to the lions in great public spectacles, crucifying them en masse, blaming them for the burning of Rome, burning them alive, and much else that sadistic imaginations employed at good salaries by the powers that be were able to come up with. As a result, the writers of that book called that empire the "anti-Christ," a "whore," a "beast," and much else that is hardly fit to print.

In that book, the shadow side of superpowering is named, and the very essence of that book is to set the champions of empire and superpowering up against "the Christ," who alone rules the world and does so by standing for healing, justice, and compassion for the poor and oppressed.

Strange to tell, many of those in Washington pushing most fanatically for the American empire today ally themselves with the Bible and with the book of Revelation itself. This use/misuse/abuse of scripture to support one's passion for power is not a new thing (Inquisitors indulged themselves in this and more in the good old days when church and state were even more muddled than they are today).

Some might argue: Well, history and fate have rendered the United States the superpower at this time, and so we must be about the business of making the world safe for McDonald's and Taco Bell and Kentucky Fried Chicken to export their (admittedly fat-producing) foods on a global basis. And this is "freedom."

When the president extols "freedom" and says that is what we are exporting around the globe, as well as our reason for making war on Iraq, I have to ask what he means by freedom. Freedom for whom? For polluters to pollute? For the rich to get richer at the expense of the poor? Freedom for the adults of this generation to leave a mess for the children of the next generation? Freedom for companies to move their headquarters to Bermuda so that they don't have to pay income taxes (while individuals stay and pay income taxes)? Freedom for cigarette manufacturers to push their dangerous wares among young teenagers in Southeast Asia (having been forbidden to advertise at home to American teenagers)? Freedom for fast-food companies to go anywhere in the world to sell their toxic and fat-making food to all cultures so they will be as obese, overweight, and sickly as ours? Freedom for drug companies to charge six hundred times their costs for prescription drugs? Freedom for drug companies who contribute to political campaigns not to be sued for putting drugs on the market that render children autistic?

A superpower must be super in its capacity to criticize itself and learn and speak the truth. How well are we doing?

To take on the mantle of "superpower" is to presume that we have something colossal to share with the rest of the world. But as I consider these facts derived from the most recent U.S. Census Bureau report on poverty and income in America I do not see much that deserves to be exported:

- The number of Americans living in poverty grew 1.3 million in 2001 to 32.9 million people.
- The most affluent fifth of the population received 50 percent of all household income while the poorest fifth shared 3.5 percent of all income.
- A former Kmart chief executive officer (CEO) received $23 million in compensation over a two-year period. The company filed for bankruptcy in 2002, and 22,000 employees lost their jobs and received no severance pay.

- A former Tyco CEO made nearly $467 million in salary, bonuses, and stock during his four years of managing a company while the shareholders lost $92 billion.
- The CEOs of twenty-three large companies under investigation by the U.S. Securities and Exchange Commission (SEC) earned 70 percent more than the average CEO and "earned" $1.4 billion between them while their companies, collectively, lost 73 percent of their wealth, or $500 billion, and laid off more than 160,000 workers.
- A Wal-Mart CEO received more than $17 million in total compensation in 2001 at the same time that employees in thirty states are suing the company because their managers forced them to punch out after eight hours of work but to continue working without pay. (The Fair Labor Standards Act says that employees must be paid time and a half for overtime.)
- More than one million corporations and individuals in the United States have registered as citizens of Bermuda to avoid paying taxes. The Internal Revenue Service (IRS) estimates this drains a minimum of $70 billion from the United States treasury— yet the IRS okays this practice.
- A poor person who qualifies for the earned income tax credit has a 1 in 47 chance of being audited, whereas those who make more than $100,000 have a 1 in 208 chance of being audited.
- In 2000, the average CEO made more in one day than

the average worker made all year. In 2000, 25 percent of all workers earned less than poverty-level wages.

- Between 1990 and 2000, the average pay for CEOs rose 571 percent; during the same period, the average worker's pay rose 37 percent.
- Forty million Americans have no health insurance, and America's largest not-for-profit health maintenance organization has just raised its premiums 24 percent.

Now tell me: Is this a superpower's values that deserve being exported anywhere at all? Is it possible to be a "superpower" and not run on a superiority complex? Is it possible to be a "superpower" and still commit to justice and compassion?

The word for "power" in Latin is *virtus,* or virtue. Virtue is the real power that humans possess. Military might is meant only as a means to defend virtue or true strength. The ultimate social virtue is justice. It is *not* the aggrandizement of power. Power is not for power's sake. It is for the community's sake—which today means the earth's sake. It follows, then, that a true superpower would be superbly virtuous, super in virtue—especially the virtue of justice. How are we doing? How are we doing regarding eco-justice? Economic justice? Gender justice? Racial justice?

Gore Vidal summarized the currently reigning cultural scene of the American superpower with the following sentence: "The same people own the media that own the White House that own the Congress that own the oil fields. They all work together to give a false view of the world to the American people."

I believe Vidal hits the nail on the head. It is a false view of the world that the American people possess, and there is a deliberate effort to keep Americans dumb. Willful ignorance and greed are considered spiritual sins in every spiritual tradition I know of. They go together very nicely. The American media sell us both. And very often our politicians climb on board for the ride.

We have a so-called democracy where 70 percent of the eligible voters either don't register or don't vote. Do we want to export that?

The truth is that for all our rhetoric about exporting freedom and democracy, we seem to live not in a democracy but in a plutocracy. *Webster's Dictionary* defines the latter as follows: "Government by the wealthy; a wealthy class that controls a government; a government or state in which the wealthy rule." Democracy is a spiritual thing, a participatory effort requiring virtue, debate, intelligence, and modesty. Plutocracy fits a superpower much more readily; it is far more efficient: government of the few, by the few, and for the few.

Is the United States exporting democracy or plutocracy? An oil plutocracy? America is the world leader in the awful linking of media, money, and government. (In my state of California, the winner in the recent gubernatorial election raised $65 million, while he was governor, to win the election. And of course the ever-hungry media—to whom it seldom occurs to offer free debate time—took in most of that money happily while complaining mildly about the corruption going on.) We have unsolved issues of racism, of genocide toward indigenous peoples, of incarceration of minority youth, of lousy schools, of regulatory bodies that don't do their job, such as the overseers of the SEC and the Department of Energy who slept through the great fleecing of California two years ago when energy prices rose 300 percent. (Maybe you have heard of Enron by now. And Anderson. And WorldCom. And dozens more.)

We *do* have alternatives to the current version of capitalism, but you would never know it judging from the inane punditry served up on CNN and Fox and other media—which, of course, are owned by winners in the current economic game. The champions of a justice-oriented and compassionate economics are nowhere to be seen or heard on our media. Consider David Korten's work, for example, which shows us the way to move from a "suicide economy" to a "living economy."

Of course, we also have alternatives to the current version of transportation in which our SUVs are gobbling up the dwindling supplies of fossil fuels. Hybrid-mix engines do work and do get 100 plus miles per gallon—and yes, someday we will probably run on totally clean hydrogen fuels. But it does not look as if Superpower America will lead the way on that issue. Maybe technology from Japan and Europe will teach us how to replace dirty fuels with clean ones if we are patient enough to wait.

To the rest of the world today, I plead as follows: Please, please—for God's sake—do not imitate America in the following categories:

- Our voting record and the system of "to the big money go the winners" (the sick notion that corporations are people with the same rights ascribed to people by the Bill of Rights—a notion that our founding fathers rejected but a late-nineteenth-century Supreme Court decision enacted)

- Our educational system
- Our penal system and justice system
- Our tax system
- Our political system
- Our economic system
- Our eating habits
- Our television
- Our disregard for the environment

I think we Americans should mend our own home before we go out into the world to convert others. I think we should be very cautious, very humble, when we reach out to other nations. Our attitude ought not to be "We are here to save you" but rather "We are in this together. What do we have to learn from one another?"

Is a country that constitutes 4 percent of the world's population but consumes 28 percent of the world's goods called to be a superpower at this time? Is a country that constitutes 4 percent of the world's population but uses 64 percent of the world's illicit drugs called to be a superpower at this time? Is a country numbed by power and media and money called to be a superpower at this time? I hope not. For all our sakes.

America Is a Light in This Dark World

DENNIS PRAGER

"No other country approaches America as a force for good on planet Earth. If a meteor destroyed the United States at this time, the world would be overrun by cruelty. The world needs a policeman, just as individual countries need policemen. And humanity should thank God every day that it is the United States of America that has the power and the moral will to be the world's policeman, and not France or China or Russia or any other country."

—Dennis Prager

Editors' note

Should America act as the world's policeman? Dennis Prager says an emphatic "yes" and thanks God for it—literally. The Jewish theologian and nationally syndicated radio talk show host minces no words when it comes to his belief in the rightness of America's mission to be a force for good in the world. God has given this country the moral responsibility to confront evil, and we must do so even if we stand alone.

Prager makes a strong argument for the divine mandate of America's dominant role as superpower. From the nation's founding, he says, we have been a Judeo-Christian country, not a secular country. America is founded on a religious perspective that embraces the idea of objective good and evil—and determines our national policy as a way to fight on the side of God. Yet our unique strength has been our ability to create the most open and tolerant society in the world, where our leaders take their oaths on both the Jewish and Christian Bibles, and our fundamental faith is in each individual's right to liberty.

America is God's chosen nation, says Prager. The rest of the world may appease or ignore the evil that abounds, but America may not. Our light must shine through the darkness.

America Is a Light in This Dark World
Dennis Prager

I believe that the United States of America has a divine mandate to be a shining light to mankind. Let me put it even more plainly. I believe that America is a chosen nation just as I believe that the Jews are God's chosen people. I also believe that while compared to its highest ideals America has often failed, compared to other countries America has indeed been a shining light.

No other country approaches America as a force for good on planet Earth. If a meteor destroyed the United States at this time, the world would be overrun by cruelty. The world needs a policeman, just as individual countries need policemen. And humanity should thank God every day that it is the United States of America that has the power and the moral will to be the world's policeman, and not France or China or Russia or any other country.

In my lifetime alone—and I was born after World War II, when America led the fight against German Nazism and Japanese Fascism—America led the fight, with little support, against Communist totalitarianism, and it now leads the fight, again with little support, against Islamic and Arab totalitarianism.

The United States, virtually alone, defends the tiny country of Israel. Why does it do so? Is it because of Jewish influence on American politicians? Cynics say so, but it is a charge that cannot be factually sustained. The American presidents most supportive of Israel (such as George W. Bush) have often come from the party that gets almost no

Jewish support, and the least supportive presidents (such as Jimmy Carter) have come from the party for which the great majority of Jews vote and to which they give enormous monetary and moral support. Moreover American Jews are not overwhelmingly pro-Israel. Many are Jews by birth but leftist by conviction and by identity, and leftist ideology is as anti-Israel as it is anti-American (for similar reasons).

The United States, virtually alone, opposes that international appeaser of evil, the United Nations. Just as this essay was being written, the United Nations Commission on Human Rights voted Libya as its chairman. For those who believe that the "international community" or "world opinion" are better arbiters of good and evil than the United States of America, such actions should bring on cognitive dissonance, if not an outright change of mind. But I suspect that most of those who believe that international opinion and its institutional embodiment, the United Nations, are more accurate moral compasses than America will ignore such as a travesty. Yet who can deny that naming Libya, a terror-sponsoring one-man dictatorship, as head of world human rights is identical to naming a serial rapist head of a committee on women's equality?

That vote in the United Nations is highly instructive. Every one of the seven European countries on the Human Rights Commission abstained (only the United States, Canada, and, it is believed, Guatemala voted against Libya). Diplomats, according to the *International Herald Tribune*, did not want to offend the African countries, whose turn it was to nominate the new chairman of the Human Rights

Commission. But why was America, which led the opposition to Libya by demanding a vote for the first time since the commission was founded in 1946, prepared to alienate the African countries and the Arab world?

Because America believes it has a moral role to play in the world, whereas Europe (not to mention China, Russia, and Japan) cares about politics and business contracts. Because America divides the world primarily into moral categories, while Europe and the others mock it for doing so. Because America believes in confronting evil, and Europe believes in appeasing it. Because America believes in itself, while Europe believes in international bodies.

Why all these differences? Because America is essentially a religious country—indeed it is by far the most religious industrialized democracy in the world.

But America is not only religious; it is religious in a unique way. It is the only Judeo-Christian country in world history. There are, and have been, many Christian countries. There are many secular countries. But only America is Judeo-Christian, and it has always seen itself as such, even though the actual term was coined in the late nineteenth century.

America was founded by Christians who were very different from the Christians of Europe. They were freedom-loving Christians and they were Jewish-oriented Christians. The founders of America revered the Jews' Old Testament and were often more preoccupied with that Testament than with the New. They named their cities after Old Testament cities, and they gave their children Hebrew names (for example, Benjamin Franklin and Cotton [meaning "small or younger"] Mather). They saw themselves as replicating the Jews' exodus from Egypt. Thomas Jefferson, the least theologically orthodox of the founders, recommended that the great seal of the United States be a depiction of the Jews crossing the sea leaving Egypt—just as America's Christians had crossed the sea from their Egypt, Europe.

And this Promised Land was to be "a shining light on a hill," in the words of a seventeenth-century leader.

But what about slavery? Doesn't that institution negate any American claims to a moral mission, let alone negate any claim to being a morally elevated culture?

No, it does not. Virtually every society in history allowed slavery. What distinguished America, therefore, was not that it had slaves, but that it was founded on ideals that made slavery ultimately unacceptable. It was a "self-evident truth" to the writers of the Declaration of Independence that "all men are created equal and endowed by their Creator with certain inalienable rights." All men, not all white men.

Moreover Americans shed more blood in a civil war to end slavery than in all their other wars combined. To those who say that the Civil War was not fought over slavery, one can only recommend that they read the proclamation of every Southern state that seceded. Each one seceded in order to protect slavery. Hundreds of thousands of white Americans died in a war fought over the humanity of black Americans.

From the Declaration of Independence citing the "Creator" to the inauguration of every American president with his hand on the Jewish and Christian Bibles to the ritual of American leaders ending their speeches with the words, "God bless America," America has been more God-oriented than any other major modern country. Moreover it has achieved something unique in history. America has had deeply religious, often "fundamentalist," Christians in power—yet these people created the most open and tolerant society in the world. Only American Christians have been able to mesh religious exclusivity and tolerance. Other tolerant societies are secular, and other religious societies are intolerant. Just to cite one simple example, every president has mentioned God in his inaugural address, but not one has mentioned Jesus. Yet they were all Christians. They were religious, God-based men who did not impose their religion.

Americans' affirmation of Judeo-Christian values, their belief that America is a Chosen Nation, and their belief in liberty (personal liberty and free markets) are the primary sources of America's greatness. They are also the sources of the hostility America engenders. Many fundamentalist Muslims hate America because it is a combination of the two religions that prevent them taking over world, which is the goal of all Islamists. Many leftists in America and Europe are anti-American because America is the world's most powerful nation while being religious and capitalist, the two ideologies that America's secular enemies loathe most.

America's differences with Europe are very instructive in this regard. America is religious; Europe is secular. Therefore, America believes morality comes from God; there is an objective good and evil, and that must guide a nation's policies. Secular Europe (and much of secular

America) believes that morality is relative and therefore international agreements, not a transcendent morality, should guide a nation's policies. Thus, Europe and its ideological brethren in America (found among the intellectual elites who are far more comfortable in Paris than in Dallas) believe that American foreign policy should be guided by the United Nations, not by Judeo-Christian notions of good and evil.

America believes in destroying evil; Europe believes in negotiating with it. This is true both internationally and domestically. Hence, Old Testament–oriented America believes that not all murderers deserve to live, while Europe and its ideological fellow travelers in America believe that all murderers should be kept alive. Europe has no problem with the Libyan dictatorship sitting at the head of the UN Human Rights Commission; America fights against it.

America believes that little Israel needs to be supported in its battle for survival against those who wish to annihilate the Jewish state. Europe believes that America and Israel are the problem, not Hamas, Islamic Jihad, and the Islamists.

Americans reproduce and take in immigrants, many of whom share their values. Europeans do not reproduce— the purpose of life for most secular Europeans (and Americans) is to have fun, and children are a real pain— and Europe will either have a civil war with its immigrants, most of whom loathe the West, or it will peacefully become Muslim. America will survive and thrive as the Judeo-Christian society it has always been. Unless the Americans who wish to destroy that identity prevail.

Is America Losing Its Soul?

TONY CAMPOLO

"The Bible calls upon great nations to humble themselves, and we should become humble if we want to be partners with the rest of the world.... What if America leaned on scripture for its foreign policy?... The Lord requires of us that we do justice and that we love mercy, and that we walk humbly with our neighbors. Would to God that this becomes our national policy."

—Tony Campolo

Editors' note

In nearly everything he does, Tony Campolo walks a fine line that allows him to speak with authority to conservative and evangelical Christians, on one hand, and to a much wider audience, on the other. A friend and former advisor to President Bill Clinton, Campolo is no stranger to issues of global importance.

His message, fully within the context of his faith, calls for the United States as a nation to be humble before God. Campolo's vision is of a God intimately involved in human affairs, with the power and inclination to bring judgment on a nation when it is deserved. Campolo refers to stories from the Hebrew Bible that demonstrate a God such as this. Then, referring to the Christian scriptures, he reflects: "In Matthew 25, Jesus tells us that all the nations of the world will be judged at the end of history according to how they have responded to the needs of the poor and the oppressed. We as Americans had better heed that warning." Even within the context of his faith—compared with what is most often preached from Christian pulpits throughout this country on Sunday mornings—Campolo's message is radical. He concludes: "What I am suggesting is that the most powerful nation on the face of the earth seek guidance from scripture. Jesus instructed us to overcome evil with good. The scriptures go on to teach us that if our enemy hungers we should feed him, and if he is naked we should clothe him, and if he is sick we should minister unto him."

Is America Losing Its Soul?
Tony Campolo

All of us readily agree with Lord Acton's famous dictum: "Power tends to corrupt and absolute power corrupts absolutely." It would be naïve for America to assume that we are above being corrupted by the wealth and the power that has fallen into our hands. It would be the utmost in arrogance to assume that we are above the temptation of having our enormous power distort the soul of our country. We can avoid such distortion and corruption, but it will require of us an incredible amount of insight into our existential situation and tremendous willpower to create a sense of godly humility among our people.

Americans do not realize that the wealth we have gained since the middle of the twentieth century has slowly made us into a very selfish people. We know that after World War II we helped rebuild Europe under the Marshall Plan, and we still think that the same kind of generosity marks our present-day foreign policy. That is not the case. Of the twenty-two industrialized nations of the world, the United States is dead last in per capita giving to the poor peoples of the world. By way of comparison, let me point out that on a per capita basis, for every dollar that America gives to the poor of the world, the people of Norway give seventy.

There are many reasons for the demise of our willingness to be generous, not the least of which is the way we have seen money squandered by dictators of Third World nations who have been the recipients of our generosity. We have seen tyrants like Mobutu in Africa take hundreds of millions of dollars of American taxpayers' money and put it into Swiss banks, or use it to build military machines to oppress their own people. Sickened by such extravagance and such immorality, we have pulled back from being a giving people. But we need to take a second look at all that squandered money and ask ourselves some serious questions. Was it not because we were irresponsible in the giving of that aid? Were we not trying to buy the allegiance of potentates of Third World nations during the Cold War years in order to keep them out of the sphere of Soviet influence? We knew what they were doing with the money but gave it to them anyway, believing that such was the price we had to pay to keep them within our camp of the politically loyal. The needs in today's world require that we recover our lost sense of generosity and respond to the many crises that now exist in the Third World.

Today the AIDS crisis is sweeping across Africa, and we in America, who have the financial means to attack that problem, have done very, very little. Presently 40 million Africans are HIV positive, and 13 million children in Africa have been orphaned because of the ravages of the AIDS epidemic. It is possible to cut back the death rate from AIDS because we have medicines that can retard the development of the HIV virus. But American pharmaceutical companies have put the price of those medicines up so high that they far exceed the capacity of poor nations to make them affordable to their citizens. Of course, the pharmaceutical companies are entitled to a fair profit, considering the enormous investments they have made in research and development, but any honest survey of those costs and the costs of distributing those medicines will demonstrate that the profits they make are exorbitant. To withhold the help that tens of millions of Africans desperately need because of the lust for unjust profits is evil.

A few years back, the United States canceled the debts that were owed us by the nation of Uganda. We did so with the stipulation that the money that would have been used to pay off the debt be specifically earmarked to attack the AIDS crisis in that country. A massive program of education and medical care was introduced. Within three years, the incidence of new cases of AIDS in Uganda was cut in half, and the incidence of deaths was diminished by almost 30 percent. The generosity of a rich country like ours can make a difference to a poor country, and Uganda is evidence of that fact. We can make a difference for good.

On September 11, 2001, three thousand innocent people were doomed to death by evil suicide bombers who flew planes into buildings in New York and in Washington, D.C. Properly, America went into mourning, and we have not yet recovered from the shock and sorrow of what happened on that horrendous day. However, we should also note that on September 11, 2001, as on any other day, more than 30,000 children in Third World countries died of starvation or diseases related to malnutrition. Those 30,000 deaths do not make our newspapers. There are no front-page stories on them. They die—and their parents not only mourn but grow angry at the richest nation on the face of the earth, which can prevent these deaths if we will to do so.

President Bill Clinton moved America in the right direction when, at the Cologne G7 Conference, which brought together leaders of the most developed countries of the world, he called for a concerted effort to end Third World debts. He saw that the poor nations of the world in Africa, Latin America, and Asia would never escape from their poverty and be able to address their social and economic problems unless the huge debts that they had incurred with the World Bank, the International Monetary Fund, and the World Trade Organization were canceled. (As a case in point, for every dollar that is paid in taxes in Ecuador, 60¢ is used not to provide health care, education, or other social services but to pay for interest—and only the interest—on debts owed by that country to those international financial organizations and to private banks throughout the rich countries of the world.) This gave birth to the Jubilee 2000 program, in which churches in developed nations lobbied their governments to engage in debt cancellation. It achieved some limited success.

If the religious community continues to utilize its influence and carry on the work of Jubilee 2000, it could bring about the change of policies by our government, as well as the governments of other rich nations, to facilitate debt reduction. This is an absolute necessity if the poor countries are to escape from their privation. The Bible tells us that to whom much is given, much is expected.

Consequently, whenever we count the blessings that we as Americans enjoy, we must recognize that with those blessings come incredible responsibilities. Thousands of years ago, God condemned the city of Sodom because, according to Ezekiel 16:49–50, its people lived in luxury while exercising indifference to the poor and oppressed. The Bible says that Sodom forgot the widows and the orphans in their affliction, and God therefore rained down judgment upon that city. Might not that same God bring the same judgment upon the United States if we follow the same path as Sodom in the years that lie ahead?

In Matthew 25, Jesus tells us that all the nations of the world will be judged at the end of history according to how they have responded to the needs of the poor and the oppressed. We as Americans had better heed that warning.

The awesome military power that we have at our disposal has led us into a reckless adventurism that threatens the future of the entire world and undermines our own security. Yet, in spite of all our military prowess and sophisticated technology, we find ourselves incredibly vulnerable. September 11, 2001, proved once and for all that we can do little in the way of defending ourselves militaristically against terrorism. We know that the components of an atomic bomb could easily be assembled in a yacht, sailed up the East River, and, by remote control, set off to blow metropolitan New York to smithereens. We realize that we can do little to prevent such a scenario. Consequently, we must recognize that the only security we can have for our future is dependent on the friends we make with other countries, especially Third World countries. We must depend on such friendships rather than on the armies that we can deploy.

If we stop to think about it, none of us really believes that we can win the war on terrorism by flexing our military might. We all know that we cannot get rid of terrorism by killing terrorists, any more than we can get rid of malaria by killing mosquitoes. We get rid of malaria by eliminating the swamps that breed the disease-carrying mosquitoes, and we will get rid of terrorism only by eliminating the conditions that breed terrorists. America has used its military might in ways that have left the Muslim world humiliated and overcome with a sense of powerlessness. That humiliation and the poverty that is all too evident among our Arab brothers and sisters have bred the terrorism that undermines our security. Recognizing such realities is the beginning of wisdom that can make for a safer world.

The time has come for the most powerful nation on the face of the earth to listen to its sister nations in the Third World. The people in those places see what we are doing in the Middle East, Iraq, and Afghanistan as nothing more than a play for control over oil reserves. Whether or not that is true is not the point. What is true in the imagination is true in the consequences. These people contend that Saudi Arabia, which has been a major source of our oil, is becoming increasingly unfriendly toward the United States and that our leaders know that our future relations with Saudi Arabia are rife with uncertainty. Those people in the Third World think that the United States, in order to shore up its oil supply, has gone into Afghanistan and is now making plays for Iraq. They note that Uzbekistan has the greatest deposit of oil anywhere in the world but that it is a landlocked nation. The only way to get the oil out of Uzbekistan is to build an oil pipe through Afghanistan. Thus, our conquest of Afghanistan is seen as a means to gaining access to Uzbekistan's oil.

Iraq controls 10 percent of the world's oil. So, when its ambassador to the United Nations tells the nations of the world that America wants to take over his country in order to gain control of its oil, we might laugh it off—but the rest of the world, especially the Third World, does not.

Immediately after the tragedies of September 11, 2001, we had the sympathy of the world on our side. I happened to be in Buenos Aires on that day, and four days later I witnessed 500,000 people assembled in the center of that capital of Argentina, praying for God's help for America. That goodwill has been squandered since then by the ways in which we have behaved. We have lost the goodwill not only of the Argentinean people but of most of the peoples of the rest of the world.

Tony Blair is working overtime to keep the United Kingdom committed to supporting United States foreign policy in the Middle East, but he's having a hard time because the overwhelming proportion of the British people see America as an arrogant bully. And when we say to the rest of the world that we don't care what they think or what they do when it comes to our foreign policy, we send a very bad message that only elicits contempt. The Bible calls upon great nations to humble themselves, and we should become humble if we want to be partners with the rest of the world.

Most Americans are unconscious of the way the political landscape has changed in the past few years. Samuel Huntington, in his book *A Clash of Civilizations,* points out that in the last half of the twentieth century, wars were primarily fought over political ideologies. In one militaristic struggle after another, the issue was whether communism or democratic capitalism would prevail. Huntington then goes on to point out that in the past three years, wars are no longer over political or economic ideologies but instead are over religious ideologies. Whether we consider the struggles of Indonesia, the civil war in the Philippines, the conflicts between Pakistan and India, or what is going on between Israel and the Palestinians, we see the same scenario. The wars are over religion. The prime minister of Egypt warns that America appears to be going to war against Islam, and we must consider the ramifications of that. There are a billion Muslims in today's world, and they have a sense of loyalty to one another that we Americans cannot possibly understand.

Sociologists since Émile Durkheim have known the power of collective religious rituals. Durkheim taught us that religious rituals, performed with great regularity, create intense communal solidarity. Now consider the fact that every Muslim in the world, five times a day, gets on his knees and bows toward Mecca in prayer, saying the same words over and over again. That collective ritual, according to Durkheim's theory, creates such an awesome sense of unity and oneness that our missionaries have had a very hard time converting anyone away from the Muslim faith. That is because the loyalty of Muslims to what they believe, and to the community of which they are a part, is regularly revitalized through their collective rituals. Consequently, we must face the fact that a war with Iraq undoubtedly would create a unified reaction from Muslims around the world against the West in general and against America in particular. The moderates in Muslim countries would soon be radicalized and join up with the likes of Osama bin Laden, and he would have achieved a victory beyond his wildest imagination.

What I am suggesting is that the most powerful nation on the face of the earth seek guidance from scripture. Jesus instructed us to overcome evil with good. The scriptures go on to teach us that if our enemy hungers we should feed him, and if he is naked we should clothe him, and if he is sick we should minister unto him.

What if America leaned on scripture for its foreign policy? What if, instead of using an embargo against Iraq, we were to provide food for its starving children and medicine for its sick? The humanitarian leaders of the United Nations have pointed out that more than half a million children have died in Iraq as a direct consequence of the embargo. Malnutrition and lack of medicine have ravished the population. The embargo, which was supposed to get the people to grow angry with Saddam Hussein and get them to rise up against him, has instead generated incredible hatred toward America. Our future does not bode well in the light of that reality. What if we were to turn all of that around by living out the instruction of Jesus and blessing those who now curse us? Might we make friends with the people of Iraq by helping them?

One philosopher of history said, "Whom the gods would destroy, they first make drunk with power." Is America being made drunk by its power, and does that drunkenness spell eventual doom in the years that lie ahead?

There can be no peace in the world without justice, and we as a superpower must work for justice. Instead of playing to special-interest groups that will ensure the election of politicians, we must work for justice in the Middle East, guaranteeing the Palestinian people as much justice as we want for the Israeli people. We must work for justice in Afghanistan. And we must seek peace with our enemies.

The Lord requires of us that we do justice and that we love mercy, and that we walk humbly with our neighbors. Would to God that this becomes our national policy.

Part 2
Making Change through Our Lives

Things Are Not What They Seem to Be— Nor Are They Otherwise

LAMA SURYA DAS

"The Dalai Lama told President Clinton, in a private meeting at the White House in the early 1990s: 'You are the most powerful man in the world. Every decision you make should be motivated by compassion.' In reality, each of us is the most powerful person in our own world. We too would do well to follow this audacious advice."

—Lama Surya Das

Editors' note

Lama Surya Das takes seriously the timeless Buddhist concepts of interconnectedness and karmic cause and effect in considering what America's role at the beginning of the twenty-first century should be. The most fortunate country in the world has the opportunity to become an example of mindful contemplation and selfless, compassionate action, he says. America can explore and develop other options beyond our dualistic, adversarial ways of relating to the rest of the world. We can learn to eschew power politics in favor of a policy of compassionately responsive wisdom and generosity.

Enriching his own direct, personal writing with teachings of the Buddha and of spiritual leaders such as Mahatma Gandhi, Lama Surya Das is in a unique position to comment on the American experience. His study of Buddhism for the past thirty years and his role as one of the foremost Western teachers of meditation allow him to contemplate the path of Buddhist practice to resolve the problems of our culture. Can America follow the Middle Way, avoiding extremes and recognizing our place in the greater web of this world and its inhabitants? Do we have a genuine teaching moment open to us now?

Things Are Not What They Seem to Be—Nor Are They Otherwise
Lama Surya Das

"Nothing is like it seems, but everything is exactly like it is."

—Yogi Berra

Things are not what they seem to be, nor are they otherwise. This is an ancient Buddhist mind-bender from the Lankavatara Sutra. Chewing on such a conundrum can help us break out of our habitual thinking and dualistic, conceptual framework. It reminds us to think outside of the box, and that everything we think we know as certain can be questioned and is subject to change.

We can observe this nowhere better than in the world of politics, scientific knowledge, and media, especially in the current world situation. We are continually reminded that everything we think we know can be questioned, and that all assertions can be logically undermined—even the one I've just made. Doesn't scientific progress teach us this to revise our thinking, even about basic principles and assumptions, every few decades? These are learning moments, cracks in the solidity of the foundations of our knowledge, which can help us loosen our tight grip on our own precious opinion—which, we are forced to remember, is based mainly on our own picture of things, which is, of course, based on the story we have told ourselves or have been told.

It would behoove all of us to try to remember the ancient yet timeless spiritual adage: If we knew the whole story, there'd be a lot less to be angry about. In fact, this line of questioning has become one of my favorite practices. When I've asked myself how to enlarge my story or my perception of things, the answer I've received is to simply enhance my understanding of the other side of the story. Simple to say, harder to do.

How many of our government officials—or any government's officials today—really understand the sociopolitical crises we face or its historical origins? The answer appears to be: not many. And yet, everyone already has an answer! Those in power become quickly entrenched in the mentality of good versus evil, right versus wrong, kill or be killed, while the situation desperately requires much more profound and subtle ways of seeing. How is it that so much, if not most, of the world veers either into one extreme or another? On one side, postmodern cynicism and disbelief. On the other, its kissing cousin: extreme fundamentalist religious views and beliefs. Is there no other way, no middle way? Are there not other lanes on the great highway of intellectual thought and conscious awareness?

Once, a snake approached the Buddha. The snake told the Enlightened Teacher, who was well known for his kindness and gentleness as well as his sagacity, that he was being harassed by village children, who threw sticks and stones at the snake whenever he slithered around hunting for food. The Buddha advised the snake not to strike back and harm the children, who knew not what they were doing. Inspired by the Buddha's beatific presence and kind heart, the snake vowed to follow that advice, and he wound his way back to his home. A few days later, the snake returned. He could hardly slither, as he was crushed and beaten bloody. Complaining to the Buddha, he said, "They beat me bloody, but—as you instructed—I did nothing in return. I accepted the abuse and barely escaped with my life." The Buddha replied, "Oh, poor snake: I did not tell you not to hiss!"

We live in dangerous times. We are capable of eradicating ourselves many times over from the face of the planet. Yet, life is sacred and worth protecting; who in his or her right mind wants to squander or destroy it? This turbulent moment in history provides us with an excellent opportunity for prayer and inner reflection. Within the paradoxes of modern life, we can use our practice to help us achieve the clarity of wisdom, unselfishness, harmony, and restraint. What better time to strive mightily to envision positive outcomes and to find and uphold the high ground? For, as the proverb says, where there is no vision the people shall perish.

One such vision is this: We need to seriously contemplate what it is we treasure most in life, and strive to realize that treasure. To do so implies that we consider where our long-term benefits and goals lie as well as continuously refocus ourselves to keep our bearings—all the while maintaining the higher ground. Gandhi called this *satyagraha*, which translates as "soul force" and/or "truth force." With his powerful observance of nonviolence *(ahimsa)* and dynamic-passive resistance, he used *satyagraha* to break the grip of the world's greatest empire.

Today we too need thoughtful reflection at the helm of our nation to further the aims of autonomy and freedom around the world. And we, the most powerful nation on earth, need to do this without eschewing the higher ground of our responsibilities and obligations to the entire interdependent world community.

If we are going to have more intelligently nuanced public conversation, we need both international and local leaders with open minds and hearts, with historical perspective and international experience. We need truth-tellers of vision and integrity. I am all too often disappointed in the shortsightedness, the meretricious moralism, and the self-interestedness of our current leaders, who often seem less like statesmen and national leaders and more like corporate flacks—shortsighted, self-righteous, anachronistic cold warriors intent on imposing an outdated worldview and cultural hegemony on a diverse, protean world. This is a sad state of affairs, which bodes ill for the future.

Whatever happened to the ideal of ethics in politics? Today there is a great sense of disillusionment in our land; too often it seems that there is no longer any bottom line other than getting elected. We are missing incorruptible moral leadership, as everyone knows, and suffering the consequences of that lack. Is it too much to ask for more civil, responsible, and enlightened leadership rather than brutish, partisan politics? Only thirty-five years ago, Robert F. Kennedy called politics "an honorable profession," and no one snickered. Almost no one. What has happened to that brand of idealism in America today? Where has that elusive spirit at the heart of authentic politics and statecraft, which Robert Greenleaf so aptly termed "servant leadership," flown to?

If we want a better world for both today and tomorrow—
and I believe we all do—we will need to incubate better
character, deeper moral fiber, and more introspection and
conscious reflectiveness in our leaders. These men and
women need to earn our trust through the test of experience. We can all be people of vision and heart, but it is
incumbent on elected leaders to cultivate the inner fortitude, patience, and life skills to handle the complex
valences of negotiation rather than simple confrontation,
and learn how to engage in meaningful collaboration with
the world community. Gone are the days of ungainly unilateralism, of an ugly America as the five-hundred-pound
gorilla in the boardroom. At least, I hope those days of
imperial arrogance are gone.

Nor should Christianity be invoked as if it were a
superior moral and democratic force, especially with the
global capitalism and power politics that have followed in
its wake in recent centuries. If America is hated in some
parts of the world, I don't think it is because of who we are
but more for what we have done as an insensitive, domi-
nating superpower. We need to rectify that situation by
redressing certain grievances and restoring a more equi-
table balance of power.

Historically, although Buddhism has been one of the
world's most populous religions, it has for the most part
eschewed power politics, imperialism, and proselytizing.
Empires rise and fall, come and go: Rome, the Ottoman
Empire, Spain, Britain. And not unlike other major faiths,
Buddhism has been associated with the ruling class in
Tibet, China, Japan, and elsewhere, although Buddhist

countries and sects have eschewed war during its lengthy history. If and when Buddhism speaks of politics, it is only as a means toward higher harmony; when we speak of power, it is the power of truth and love, of purity, character, and integrity; of unselfish generosity and service; and of far-seeing, all-hearing, compassionately responsive wisdom. Compassion, perhaps the greatest jewel of them all, can transform the world because with it we transform ourselves and one another in ever-widening circles of connection and respect, transforming this world from the inside out.

Buddhism has never put much stock in the vagaries and vacillations of this world. The compassionate sage known as Buddha taught that the dualisms of pleasure and pain, loss and gain, fame and shame, praise and criticism are merely eight pitfalls: eight fleeting, worldly winds that merely blow us around without leading anywhere. The bodhisattva, who lives by the Ten Transcendental Virtues or Spiritual Powers—generosity, ethical self-discipline, patient forbearance and inner fortitude, fearless effort and energy, focused mindfulness, wisdom, skillful means and resource-fulness, unselfish leadership, steadfast resolve, and pristine spirituality—is the ultimate spiritual and social activist and can function when called upon as a transformational leader. He or she has been called a peaceful warrior, an awakened warrior—one who follows the Buddha's teaching that the greatest enemy and opponent lies in the egotism and delu-sion within oneself, and that he who conquers himself is the greatest of conquerors. The Sutra on Oneness and Interpenetration says, "If you want to get rid of your enemy, the true way is to realize that your enemy is delusion." The bodhisattva ideal challenges us to pick up our meditation cushions and learn to walk our talk, and become the changes that we want to see in the world.

We require new ways of seeing and being, so that we sidestep the slippery slope of autocratic, often isolationist power politics and can help to cocreate a better world with our fellow world citizens. Finding the ways by which we can do this should be the collective ongoing research project and immediate undertaking of all those who feel compelled and willing to strive toward a new world. We should be educating young people so that they learn how to learn and how to keep learning, not just how to get a degree that delivers a job and a paycheck at the end of a decade or two of schooling. We seem collectively unable to recognize the interdependence of all, just as we seem equally unable to grasp the implications of emphasizing the short-term, local interest. An ancient sage once said, "Give light, and the people will find their own way." This should be part of the credo for new forms of authentic higher education.

Is anyone thinking about where we and our world are collectively headed? Where will the world be one hundred or five hundred or one thousand years from now? As we adjudicate and legislate and vote concerning the ozone layer, industrial pollution, world water resources, nuclear waste, AIDS in Africa, and scientific research in our own supposedly free country, is anyone making decisions in the light of the unforeseeable future? Robert E. Hunter, C. Ross Anthony, and Nicole Lurie, writing in the August 2002 *Rand Review,* propose making world health the new Marshall Plan, using the power, might, and knowledge of this country to reduce suffering and death. This would indeed be a good place to begin a new era of American friendliness, inquiry, listening, and cooperation, rather than unilateralism and hegemony.

If we assume that the rest of the world wants—let alone needs—the invisible export of our American ethos, we make a dangerous mistake that will only inflame the hatred of our current enemies while also making our own allies cringe. Is the West really best? It would be a wonderful thing if the United States were to lead more by example than by force or manipulation. And now is the time. We are just now learning that millions of people have cultural and religious values that are dramatically different from ours. Is our fear-ridden, security-minded, politically divided country the happiest society on earth? Our own superconsumerism and materialism is far from a panacea; taken to extremes, it can be a powerful poison, acting like an addictive drug. I think we would do well to consider how we might live more lightly upon this good earth, pull in our belts a bit, and share more of our good fortune while taking more interest in how others live and think. Our neighbors would appreciate it.

However, our recent track record is not that positive. We use a disproportionate amount of the world's resources while at the same time removing ourselves from environmental treaties, international alliances, and organizations. We support dictatorships favorable to our temporary energy interests, changing alliances with the winds of politics and alienating countries and people who had once counted us as friends. This kind of betrayal does not endear us to others.

As we live among nations like the rich people in the hilltop mansion, we create heavy karma. How can we not? Those who live down below are human, are they not? How is it that our view of reality allows us to perceive ourselves as a model of the well-lived life—envisioning ourselves as the good guys, the decent society, the paragons of virtue, equality, liberty, and justice—while so many others in the world view us as unwilling to hear and respond in a truly compassionate way? We ought to try to look at ourselves through the eyes of others, especially those to whom we strive to "benevolently" dictate. We need to engage in politics of a new kind, recognizing our place in the greater web of this world and its inhabitants—all of its inhabitants, not merely those who look or think like us—and pull together if we don't wish to be pulled apart. This is a fact of life.

Until we clear our vision and loosen the grip of our selfish preoccupations, I fear that we will continue to be unable to intelligently and skillfully address the numerous external and internal problems that we face. How can we face the challenges of this complex time when we are stuck in what can only be seen as collective narcissism? If we wish to reduce the ignorance, illusion, greed, avarice, conflict, racism, prejudice, intolerance, and violence in the world, we need to begin by reducing it in our own hearts and minds. If, however, we are lazy, lost in the superficial beauty of our modern convenience-filled lives, we will be stuck forever. The seeds of these diseases are in you and in me, and we overlook and ignore them at our peril. However, if and when we lift the veil of illusion, selfless compassionate action naturally arises. This is universal law.

With power comes responsibility, as has been said by many different people in various parts of the world. With greatness, or even with mere largeness, should come some perspective as well. We, as the only "superpower" left in this crumbling world, must develop more sensitivity to the totality of that of which we imagine ourselves to be the linchpin. We may seem to be the world hyperpower today— but for how long? And let us rest assured, we are not the true superpower in this created universe. Any internal check with your own conscience and spirit will confirm this, any time of day or night, regardless of the news, United Nations resolutions, battles won and lost, or election results. We are merely the big kid on the block in this grade, at this stage, and locally at best. There is a greater power, however we may conceive or imagine it.

We can no longer be the world's policeman, but neither can we remain above the fray. September 11 was a painful, unwelcome reminder of that fact. We are global citizens in a global society, with global economic and environmental concerns. Overpopulation, water and air pollution, economic injustice—these are among many other issues that link the future of all our families and countries in one great, shimmering, interwoven web of inter-being. We need to assume a leadership role in the world and consider the long-term welfare and best interest of all, as well as preserving the many unique characteristics and heritages of the world's people. We need to be and act as a beacon of human rights, justice, and liberty, not as cultural imperialists who try to impose our values and culture around the world, however unconsciously or even subtly.

We need, as much as is reasonably possible, to detach our foreign aid from American political agendas and imperatives. We need to persuade others by our actions rather than by mere ideas and unactualized ideals.

Today's political process seems to suffer from lack of imagination. If we continue to frame and discuss new challenges in old terms, limiting ourselves and our possibilities to familiar frames of mind and language, we lose the possibility of sociopolitical innovation. We will never be able to have a new kind of public conversation. We need to find and explore and develop other options beyond our dualistic, adversarial ways and means. I am certainly not the first to bemoan the black-and-white, overly simplistic, us-or-them, short-term thinking and partisan mentality that seems to govern so much of our policymaking today. Is there no one astute enough to apply timeless Buddhist notions of interconnectedness and karmic cause and effect to solutions that are timely and appropriate for today and tomorrow?

Mahatma Gandhi said that there are seven blunders causing the violence that plagues the world: wealth without work, pleasure without conscience, knowledge without character, commerce without morality, science without humanity, worship without sacrifice, and politics without principles. If there are those who hate us, cause may be found in such missteps.

Gandhi also said: "I am told that religion and politics are different spheres of life. But I would say without a moment's hesitation and yet in all modesty that those who claim this do not know what religion is." He continued:

"Nonviolence, truth, nonstealing, sacred sex, nonconsumerism, physical work, avoidance of bad taste, fearlessness, respect for all religions, local economy, and respect for all beings. These eleven principles should be followed with humility, care, and commitment."

Buddha taught that finding the balance and harmony beyond extreme views and fixed opinions could be the essence of a free and liberated life. Finding a higher, or at least common, ground beyond polarization is the essence of applying the Middle Way in life. Buddhism has much to offer that is applicable to conflict resolution and reconciliation. By itself, the Buddhist contemplative and healing art of mindfulness can help bring listening to a new level, and this is crucial for any kind of dialogue or communication.

I lived for half a dozen years in a Tibetan Buddhist monastery, a forest cloister, under my late teacher's guidance. One amazing discovery for me was to find there—mirrored within those blessed, peaceful, sylvan walls and garden—much of the same dissatisfaction and delusion that can be found in the world around us. All of those conflicts and illusions lie within. The soul of man is the true battlefield, as Dostoevsky and Gandhi both said. Thus, we find many spiritual warriors dedicated to waging this inner struggle for the benefit of the world as well as for inner peace. As above, so below; as within, so without. Another discovery of equal import was how much we are all the same in what we want, need, and aspire to, one way or another, regardless of how different we may look from outside, and how we can learn to love even those we disagree with and may not always like, for love is greater than the dualism of mere like and dislike. I experienced this directly from living in extremely close contact with two dozen cloistered monks and nuns for six years.

If we want to transform the world, we must engage in it. Still, there is another world, another reality, a deeper invisible dimension where we can find enough sustenance and purpose and energy so that we will never become discouraged or exhausted. This is our innate spiritual connection, and it can sustain us through all the vagaries of life. International relations are seldom simple or easy, and innumerable crosscurrents and concerns must be considered when dealing at such a level. Yet, from the quiet and open centeredness of spiritual insight comes a flow of effective and appropriate actions. These ride the waves of constant, clear-sighted inquiry into objective facts, if such exist, combined with evolving and changing realities. I believe that bringing contemplative practice and perspectives into the corridors of power could be one of the most effective contributions any of us could make to this world.

Recently, in search of hope and inspiration, I visited the various monuments and memorials around the National Mall in Washington, D.C. I recommend this as a foot pilgrimage to all of us. It provides the opportunity for new ideas. On a beautiful autumn day, my wife and I walked from the Capitol building down the mall, past the Smithsonian and the Aerospace Museum and through the outdoor sculpture garden, to the Washington Memorial, past the White House, and on to the moving Vietnam Veterans Memorial and the Korean War Veterans Memorial, and then the Lincoln, Jefferson, and Franklin

Roosevelt monuments. Who knows how well our old icons would have withstood the baleful glare of modern media and our tell-all celebrity culture? And yet, how I long for leaders more like those of old! What are we doing to create those types of leadership qualities today? Are we creating leaders or followers through our education and socialization processes? Where will the true leaders of the future come from? Where are the protégés of Mahatma Gandhi and Martin Luther King Jr. today?

This country has been at war most of the time during the past sixty years. There are wars raging in more than forty-two countries of the world on this very day. The question, then, is not war or peace—a choice we can easily make—but war *and* peace: a far more complicated equation. The military-industrial complex and the arms industry are certainly complicit in this tangle, which is far more complex than a seeming battle between the forces of good and evil. One can learn a great deal from Michael Moore's recent documentary film on the American culture of fear and violence, *Bowling for Columbine.* "War is a crime. Ask the infantry and ask the dead," said Ernest Hemingway. If we agree that war is outmoded as a means of resolving conflict in our shrinking yet increasingly complex, pluralistic, postmodern world, we must ask ourselves: What shall we find to replace it?

My Cambridge neighbors at the Harvard Project on Negotiation, among others, have studied and documented how we can find common ground through putting ourselves in the place of the other and seeing things through the other's eyes. Their studies in negotiation and conflict resolution tell us to look and listen for what the other side needs and wants, then look and listen harder; try to learn their story; and look at our own contribution in maintaining the conflict, because this is what we can immediately take control of.

We must be realistic, neither overly optimistic nor pessimistic. I believe in the innate goodness of the heart and the magnificence of the mind. Spiritual freedom through enlightened consciousness is not a pipe dream; many have achieved it, and the means to accomplish that great goal are near at hand. There is a path to what we seek, not just a hope and a prayer. We must undertake such a path.

Personally, I will never give up. No matter how discouraging corporate corruption, political self-interest, environmental destruction, social injustice, and international terrorism and bloodletting become, I will not give up. I don't find any other way but to continue the good fight and to make it a peaceful one, throughout all my lifetimes, for the benefit of all that lives and breathes—beyond humanity and its discontents, and including all beings seen and unseen. This requires inner strength, fortitude, and commitment. We must do all that we can, especially since we never really know what will ultimately make the most difference in the direction of positive change and transformation.

Tibetan Buddhist lamas teach that the cusp of a new millennium is the most excellent and appropriate time for a personal as well as a collective moment of reflection, when we can genuinely stop and give ourselves a momentary break in order to better reflect upon and take stock of where we are, where we are coming from, and where we are going. I am trying to reprioritize my needs, desires, and intentions in the light of the fact that I will not be here forever—nor will any of us—and striving to remember the profound spiritual wisdom of learning how to love and honor even those I may not like.

September 11 was a turning point in American history. It opened the door to a genuine teaching moment, when the chink in our armor was temporarily wide open. Yet, what have we learned? Have big business, party politics, environmental protection, the media, health care, education, racism, street violence, and our penal system changed since then? Are we actually making the world a safer place—or are we making it a more dangerous one? Haven't we gone back to business as usual, both for better and for worse?

The old structures of the world are cracking apart, the moment of creative chaos is upon us, and the drama of our time has become a great question: What new principles, what new structures—social, political, economic, intellectual, psychological, spiritual—will emerge to shape our future? I think we need to clear our minds and hearts, rather than rushing forward on the treadmill of events, unable to really move under the burden of old, semiconscious habits and conditioning. We are not helpless victims or prisoners held hostage by circumstances or conditions or forces greater than ourselves. We can master ourselves and our karma, our fate and our destiny; it is not what happens to us but what we make of it that can make all the difference. We cannot control the winds of kismet, but we can learn better how to sail. The fate of the world rests in our hands.

The Dalai Lama told President Clinton, in a private meeting at the White House in the early 1990s: "You are the most powerful man in the world. Every decision you make should be motivated by compassion." In reality, each of us is the most powerful person in our own world. We too would do well to follow this audacious advice.

In Every Generation, Pharaoh

RABBI ARTHUR WASKOW

"The question is: How quickly, after how many deaths and how many plagues upon the earth itself, can the arms and legs and hands of God—the people—act? How long will it take for them to let the Spirit fill them?"

—Rabbi Arthur Waskow

Editors' note

Does God act in the world? Has God been a force in human history? For Arthur Waskow, the answer to both questions is "yes," but God acts only through the People of God. We are the eyes, ears, arms, and legs of God in the world.

"In every generation," Waskow writes, "all human beings must see themselves as those who rise to go forth from slavery to freedom." There are those who help to free slaves and those who enslave them. Which will we be?

Waskow pulls no punches. Using the story most basic to his religious tradition, he writes: "In the archetypal language of biblical tradition, this fusion of superstate [America], global corporations, and their servicing institutions [e.g., the World Bank] are Pharaoh in our generation."

The biblical Pharaoh's power was characterized by arrogance, rigidity, and conscious wrongdoing. What is needed today, according to Waskow, is for us to become agents of liberation from Pharaoh—like the biblical Moses, Miriam, and Aaron—and the first step in this direction is to recognize the unity that connects all life, that connects us to our enemies.

In Every Generation, Pharaoh
Rabbi Arthur Waskow

The Passover Haggadah, the "telling" of the story of deliverance from narrowness and slavery, has within it two passages that begin "In every generation." In every generation, one arises against us to destroy us. In every generation, all human beings must see themselves as those who rise to go forth from slavery to freedom.

In every generation, both. Some new Pharaoh will assert more tight control and deadly power over us; we must create more freedom and community among us.

WHERE IS PHARAOH IN OUR GENERATION?

Before we address this question, let us look at the depth of meaning in the assertion "In every generation." This process begins even before the human race is born. One way to describe evolutionary and human history is as a spiral from generation to generation—from greater control (over the earth and other human beings) to deeper and broader community (involving the earth and other human beings), followed by new advances in forms of control that bring on deeper and broader forms of community.

For example, the amoebas that mastered control over nearby nutriment-bearing water needed to learn to interact with other forms of life if they were not to use up all the nearby nourishment and die. They "invented" a way to become multicelled cooperative creatures—a new form of community.

Once these cooperative creatures emerged, they learned to master more of their environs. The level of control advanced. Control, I-It, bred community, I-Thou; and then community bred control. And so on. A spiral of change.

Examples in human history:

- When Western Semitic tribes (small farmers, shepherds, nomads) faced the monocrop imperial agriculture of Babylonia—a great leap in doing, control—what emerged from the economic, political, and spiritual crisis was biblical Israel: a great deepening in being and loving, community.
- When biblical Israel faced hellenization and the Roman Empire—a great leap in doing, control— what emerged from the economic, political, and spiritual crisis were Rabbinic Judaism and Christianity, and later Islam: great deepenings in being and loving, community.

This rhythm can be understood as the dance of God in the world. We are at a crisis in this rhythm again, in this generation.

Control has a way of running amok, blocking the rhythm. In the past fifty years there have emerged institutions so huge, so controlling, so global in their reach that they have to a considerable extent escaped the forms of community and connection-making that have been shaped over the past several centuries by national democratic processes. They have become major top-down unaccountable power centers.

One of these institutions is the sole surviving superstate, the United States. Its enormous wealth has become more and more concentrated in fewer and fewer hands, and this process becomes self-reinforcing as the ultrawealthy win more control over the media and the political parties. Changes in tax policy in just the past few years portend even tighter concentrations in wealth and power. So do steps to diminish the power of labor unions and to restrict civil liberties and the privacy of citizens, while increasing governmental secrecy.

Meanwhile, besides tightening control at home, a tiny elite extends its power—military, economic, and political— around the world. Although other nations have nuclear weapons, only the United States has enough such weapons, and the military infrastructure, to be able to threaten to use them in anything but deterrence or retaliation. Only the United States can send navies to several regions of the world at once.

Only the United States has the financial clout to threaten the United Nations with bankruptcy and thereby win control over its decisions. Only the United States has the economic clout in every continent to press almost all governments to follow its lead or face political and economic upheavals. And only the United States has the ability to fund destabilizing organizations and events on every continent to topple governments or punish peoples that disobey.

The only check on this power has been the danger that such upheavals would "blow back" on the United States through terrorism. So far, the American elites have treated that danger—and its brutal, bloody reality—as an occasion to tighten, not loosen, their control. So only the United States has the power to announce with impunity that it intends to not only use its power to its own advantage but use it to prevent the emergence of any alternative center of power that could threaten its control in the future.

One of the key elements in the power of the United States elites is that they are closely allied with global corporations that have themselves used their power—often secretively—to move into the political processes of many nations to reshape their political and economic systems. Out of this amalgam of state and corporation have emerged the World Bank, the International Monetary Fund, and the World Trade Organization. They have been able to bypass and negate decisions previously made in public view by the national governments.

The corporations and their servicing institutions have especially endangered decisions won by decades or even centuries of painful struggle at the national level that affirm both the basic process of public accountability and the specifics of workers' rights, environmental protections, and public health and educational services.

To put this in the archetypal language of biblical tradition, this fusion of superstate, global corporations, and their servicing institutions constitutes a pharaoh in our generation.

Pharaoh was not consciously and deliberately evil; he worried about his country, and he grew fearful that an odd and indigestible minority might make trouble for the complex pattern of its governance. The arrogance that grew inside him until he was swallowed up by it was probably rooted in the loneliness of pyramidal power. So much depended on him that he became convinced that his own wisdom was indispensable—and total.

If we look for a pharaoh in our lives today, we should be looking not for deliberate evil but for people or institutions who hold such great power that they become convinced that they are indispensable, and who are isolated from critical comment and accountability so long that when they meet it they respond chiefly with stubbornness and anger.

Out of his sense of overall responsibility to the way he understood society was supposed to run, Pharaoh ended up enslaving workers, ordering the deaths of little children, and bringing down upon his country a series of environmental disasters. (We call these eco-disasters the Ten Plagues—the pollution of Egypt's key river, the swarming of frogs and locusts, an epidemic of cattle disease, and so on.)

This much—the increasing rigidity and arrogance of unaccountable power—we may ruefully recognize in many areas of our lives: families, workplaces, whole communities, and nations—even the relationship of *Homo sapiens* to the earth in our own generation. But from this story we learn not only to understand the expectable but to embrace the unimaginable. For the story teaches that the deepest truth of the universe—God's own self—rose up against all logical expectations, using both human resistance and the rebellious earth itself to topple the greatest concentration of power in the world and to turn a bunch of runaway slaves into the beacon of history for freedom, justice, and holiness.

Our religious traditions remember not only Pharaoh: they remember also a series of such imperial powers—out of which, again against all "logic," came the birth of new religious communities that transformed the world. Both Jews and Christians remember the Roman Empire, which used its arrogant power to crucify Jesus and torture ten of the greatest rabbis to their deaths, to sow ancient Palestine with salt so that crops would not grow, and then to sell its people into slavery. Out of that oppressive addiction to control came both the new community of rabbinic Judaism and the new community of Christianity.

Muslims remember that the arrogantly powerful of Muhammad's day forced him to flee from Mecca to Medina in order to bring God's teachings to the people. Out of that resistance to control run amok came the community of Islam.

Buddhists remember that Gautama had to leave the power of the palace to understand the sufferings of the poor and to experience and teach enlightenment. The entire Buddhist worldview was born from that experience.

In the past century, many peoples came to remember that Mahatma Gandhi had to face a mighty empire to fuse the ancient insights of his people into the teachings of *satyagraha* (soul force, or nonviolence). From that experience of the Imperial Raj came the birthing of a planetary consciousness of nonviolence—a new level of community emerging from suffering under colonial control.

And one of the most poignant and powerful expansions of that community of nonviolence came in black America's response to racism and segregation. Control ran berserk in the form of police dogs, lynch mobs, and church bombings. The indigenous communities and spiritual traditions of the Americas, Africa, Asia, and Australia remember how they were shattered by arrogant political leaders in concert with arrogant economic bosses—and how their resurgence came in part from the overreaching of those rulers.

Growing numbers of women remember how the spiritual experience of women has been suffocated for millennia by the arrogance of some religious, political, and economic tyrants—and how that suffocation has itself helped spark the emergence of a creative movement seeking new forms of community among women and in society as a whole.

These are the separate streams of the separate memories of our different traditions. These different streams flow together into a great ocean of planetary outrage and planetary promise. So today, many of us remember not only "our own" but all those spiritual struggles for justice and compassion, while according special love and connection to the experiences, symbols, and histories of our own.

UNACCOUNTABLE POWER IN THE BIBLE'S EXODUS SAGA

The Egyptian king drew on the psychological and political adeptness of the outsider Joseph both to save lives and to maximize his own power in a time of famine that might otherwise have brought on mass deaths and drastically weakened the Pharaoh's authority. Joseph provided a way to make Pharaoh the owner of practically all Egyptian land, turning into sharecroppers those who had before been relatively independent yeomen. Only the priests—whose religious authority affirmed the Pharaoh as a god—preserved their economic base as landholders.

Then, says the story, a Pharaoh arose "who knew not

Joseph," who had no intimate understanding of him. Perhaps this new Pharaoh came to power precisely by bitter attacks on the "foreigners" who had helped a previous dynasty strip "real Egyptians" of their dignity and worth. Or perhaps the new Pharaoh simply saw a way to protect his power by blaming "immigrants" for public problems. Perhaps, once its power was solidified, the Egyptian monarchy turned workers—not necessarily these outsiders alone—into overburdened slaves, doing forced labor for the state.

In either case, the story says that the central government focused popular fear and hatred of its oppressive structure onto distrust and fear of these outsiders. It singled out the Hebrews (the very word, then derogatory, meant "the crossover people," "transgressors," "vagrants," "wetbacks") for a genocidal policy. What had begun as an effort to save lives during the Great Famine became, step by step, the arrogance of unaccountable power.

Pharaoh ordered midwives to murder all Hebrew boys at birth. And then we hear the first hint of rebellion against the genocidal policy. The midwives refused, and when Pharaoh assailed their failure they told him that the Hebrew women were so quick to give birth that the babies were safely born before the midwives could arrive. And when Pharaoh found other killers, a Hebrew and an Egyptian woman—Miriam and Pharaoh's daughter—conspired to save the life of one small baby: Moses.

These two stories are the first tales in recorded history of nonviolent civil disobedience. The Bible says that the midwives acted because "they revered God," but there is no tale of an audible divine intervention. Instead, we are left to understand that the midwives heard God's voice in every baby's cry, saw God's face in every parent's love.

But Pharaoh persevered. The result, according to Exodus, was that the monarchy's oppressive actions toward its people began to affect the land itself. The rivers became undrinkable, frogs and mosquitoes infested the country, climate change brought unexpected extreme weather, cattle disease struck down huge herds. As these plagues damaged the economy and shook the throne, the Pharaoh's own advisers urged him to change policy: "Are you not yet aware that Egypt is shattered?"

But his arrogance became still harsher and more brittle. Its consequences are expressed through the dramatic figure of an interventionist God who humbles Pharaoh. For Pharaoh tried to set himself apart from history, astride the earth. Again and again, he hardened his own heart, thickening the tough casing around it to keep himself separate from the suffering of Egyptians as well as of the Israelites. Finally, he became addicted to this hardening of his heart; he lost even the ability to choose whether to open his heart to others. The story explains that God's own self—the underlying process of reality—hardened Pharaoh's heart. The very alienation Pharaoh had chosen brought about his downfall.

His rigid, brittle power was engulfed by a hurricane of God's own breath and was washed away by great sea waves. Pharaoh certainly noticed the disasters that were befalling Egypt. But he rejected the notion that these disasters were a consequence of anything—certainly not a consequence of his own oppressive actions. He refused even to notice the rule of consequences, because he denied there was a unity. He denied it not just by prayers and prostrations to the many gods of Egypt but by his actions, separating himself and his power from that unity. In a world that had no flow of unity and consequence, he assumed that these disasters were a series of mere accidents.

In the Bible's archetypal tale of liberation, what made Moses, Miriam, and Aaron unusual was that they saw the disasters as a consequence of Pharaoh's oppression. They could see this because they saw the unity that connects all life. What happened to Moses at the burning bush was that this unity became visible to him.

The biblical writers gave a name—a strange name—to this unity and the process of consequences it involved. This name was "Y-H-W-H," the Breath of Life. Because it was a breathing, this name included all ordinary words and names and went beyond all ordinary names and words. This name expressed deep awe for the underlying process by which these interactive consequences were made real— and perhaps even more awe for the overarching process by which the underlying unity of consequences was made visible to human awareness.

To those who called out and wrote down the story of the Exodus, it was clear that the plagues were consequences of Pharaoh's oppressive action. It was also clear that Moses understood the law of consequences, while Pharaoh did not. And it was clear that this law of consequences sprang from the unity that underlies all life, so it was both a noticeable truth and an awesome mystery.

To the bards and writers of the Bible, the step-by-step details of this process were not known. So it was not only a mystery but a miracle. To us today, this process of consequence may no longer seem miraculous; for today we could make a well-defined socioecological analysis of how the exploitation of workers is connected with turning Oklahoma into a dust bowl or decimating the Amazon forest or pouring mercury into the Great Lakes. But for many of us today, the understanding of what no longer seems a miracle does not dissolve our sense of awe and mystery: our sense of awe in the mysterious presence of the breath that breathes all life and intertwines it. And today we still face the grim face of pharaohs who once again refuse to recognize the unity, who refuse to affirm the law of consequence, and who therefore refuse to connect onrushing disasters with their own behavior, even when their own advisers shriek at them as Pharaoh's did: "Do you not see that you are destroying our own land?"

Our biblical tradition, reinforced by many others, teaches that the arrogance of Pharaoh, of every pharaoh, ultimately becomes so rigid, so brittle, that the combination of its own alienation from reality and the will to freedom of its people and of the universe drown out its arrogance.

The midwives' heroic example, together with the midwife-mothering of Miriam and of Pharaoh's daughter, become a model for God's midwifery: *Mitzrayyim,* the narrow place that is the Hebrew word for Egypt, becomes the narrow birth canal for a new community. The birthing waters break as the People Israel is born, and those same waters wash away the stubborn Pharaoh.

The question is this: How quickly, after how many deaths and how many plagues upon the earth itself, can the arms and legs and hands of God—the people—act? How long will it take for them to let the Spirit fill them?

How long before we hear the voice of God in every baby's outcry, in the croaking of each distorted, dying frog? How long before we gently, firmly, disobey the orders, dismantle the social systems, and break the personal habits that bear the lethal seal of Pharaoh? And how long before we create new communal forms to birth new life?

Waging a Greater Jihad for America

EBOO PATEL

"Too many countries have experienced America as a predator. Too often has America lacked the courage to do the greater good and instead settled for being the lesser evil: not as racist as Nazi fascism, not as imperialist as Soviet communism, not as wanton as Islamic terrorism. At the same time, many immigrants—including those from the very countries that America has pounced on—have known America as a promise. America has provided new life to people from the four corners of the earth."

—Eboo Patel

Editors' note

An American-born Muslim of Indian ancestry not yet in his thirties, Eboo Patel lives enthusiastically in both present and past. He is equally comfortable discussing the effect of American hip-hop music on traditional Indian culture and the "trauma of contradictions" in the life of Thomas Jefferson, slaveholder and democrat. His perspective on America as superpower is divided as well. Is America a predator, he asks, or is America a promise?

Writing about his own experience in Bombay, in London, and in the great cities of the United States, Patel attempts to reconcile the dichotomy of the country that has perhaps done more damage worldwide than any other nation but has also extended the promise of a better life to millions of immigrants who have come to its shores over the centuries. What is the American tradition of righteousness? In the end, he says, it may come down to America's being "a grand gathering of souls, the vast majority from elsewhere"—and each of those souls has a history and a life. To his consideration of America's responsibilities as superpower Patel brings the stories of his Muslim soul, and he advises: "This is what we must do: Believe deeply, act boldly, begin now. Great nations are made of righteous strivings."

Waging a Greater Jihad for America
Eboo Patel

"I am a patriot
I have been fighting the good fight"
—Ani DiFranco

When I was a graduate student at Oxford a few years back, I heard British journalist Will Hutton declare that we are living in an American imperium. How peculiar, I thought, to hear the accent that shook the world only sixty years ago recognize its former colony as the new empire. England lost its dominance to America in a series of little defeats. Witness India. Upper-class students in Bombay and Delhi once dreamed of studying at Cambridge and Oxford. Now they are set on Harvard and Princeton. Enid Blyton books have given way to Archie comics and John Grisham novels. And although cricket remains India's most popular sport, American basketball, with marketing gimmicks in tow, is making furious headway.

Other examples of America in India abound. My grandmother made me take her to see *Titanic* three times when I visited her in Bombay in the summer of 1998. My Indian cousins refused to accompany us. They had already taken her to see it twice. One of Bombay's most popular clubs among the younger set of rich kids is called The Ghetto. Nineteen-year-old girls wearing tight DKNY tops rub up against nineteen-year-old boys wearing baggy Levis and Shaquille O'Neal jerseys. American glam metal music blares from the speakers, and the imitation hip-hop graffiti is illuminated with fluorescent lights. When I asked a friend from a village in Gujarat why everyone I talked to in India was so fascinated by America, he told me *Baywatch*.

Indians are not the only ones with appetites for America. Hollywood movies dominate the cinemas in London's Leicester Square and Johannesburg's Santon City Mall. Victoria's Secret and Barbie are popular in Teheran. Ten-year-old kids in Sri Lankan villages sing Backstreet Boys' songs.

Political scientists call the reach of American products part of our "soft" power. It threatens nations in a different way than our missiles do. American cultural artifacts carry American attitudes and values, many of which cut against the grain of important traditions in other societies. Barbie has a boyfriend, and the Backstreet Boys sing about seducing women, but parents in Iran and Sri Lanka might not want their children in American-style dating relationships. The *Baywatch* crew shimmy and jiggle in bathing suits, but some Indians might consider this an affront to a society that values modesty in dress. Let us remember that, whatever else they might be, Barbie, the Backstreet Boys, and *Baywatch* are money-making machines for American multinationals. Countries are justifiably proud of their cultural traditions. It should come as no surprise that people who want to protect those ways of life are unwilling to allow American marketers full access to their lands without a fight.

Like American culture, American military power covers the globe. Hundreds of thousands of American troops armed with the most advanced weaponry are stationed in nearly two dozen countries around the world. Sometimes these soldiers act recklessly—like flying six hundred feet below minimum altitude and one hundred miles per hour over the maximum speed limit through an Italian resort town and slicing a ski-lift cable that drops twenty people to their deaths. The soldiers destroyed the video evidence of their ill-advised acrobatics and were exonerated by a military court in North Carolina. We Americans acted surprised by the anger in Italy, but we never bothered to notice that there are no Italian military bases in Orlando or Duluth.

Perhaps America's might would not be so troublesome if we were not so brutally arrogant. Gruesome attacks happen around the world all the time, but no other country would have the audacity to declare a worldwide witch-hunt and threaten sympathizers and skeptics alike with the warning "You are either with us or against us." And whether or not they follow the logic of threatening a dictator years away from acquiring nuclear weapons while supporting one known to have them, other countries must put their agendas at the United Nations aside and discuss the United States' most recent hallucination. Washington twitches, and the world order shifts.

"Please call me by my true names,
so I can wake up"

—Thich Nhat Hanh

Thirty years ago, Students for a Democratic Society insisted on naming the American system. They called it imperialism. The land and people of Chile, El Salvador,

Iran, Vietnam, and several other nations that Americans can neither locate nor pronounce will attest to that. Too many countries have experienced America as a predator. Too often has America lacked the courage to do the greater good and instead settled for being the lesser evil: not as racist as Nazi fascism, not as imperialist as Soviet communism, not as wanton as Islamic terrorism.

At the same time, many immigrants—including those from the very countries that America has pounced on—have known America as a promise. America has provided new life to people from the four corners of the earth. It is true that some were forced to come, and few felt welcome when they arrived, but most decided to throw their lot in with this piece of earth. The promise of America allows them to find jobs, start businesses, buy homes, build houses of worship, create organizations, elect leaders, and reasonably expect a better life for their children. Hatreds from their histories rarely take root in American soil. Indians and Pakistanis, Bosnians and Serbs, Israelis and Palestinians—they don't murder each other in the streets of American cities.

In fact, America has often infused a healing energy into bitter enmities. Take the story of my friend Marios. Marios grew up in Greek Cyprus and, like other Greek Cypriots, thought the people who lived on the other side of the wall in Turkish Cyprus were ogres. His parents sent him to America for college, and during a summer off he went to see a dentist in New York City to take care of a toothache. Making casual conversation, the dentist asked, "Where are you from?" Marios answered, "Cyprus." "Me too," said the dentist.

They discovered that their homes were only a few miles apart in Nicosia, but on different sides of the wall in the last divided city on earth. New York City provided what Nicosia could not: an opportunity for a conversation. They went for a drink and, wary at first, began to discover each other, and themselves. Several years later, Marios returned to Nicosia to found an organization that brings Turkish Cypriot youth and Greek Cypriot youth together for summer camps. The camps are held in Vermont. The kids are cold to one another for the first few days, Marios says, but then they discover that they have a lot in common: "They all wear Nikes, listen to hip-hop, and enjoy American films."

American soil contains a spirit meant for all humanity. One does not have to cross our borders to glimpse America the promise. Ho Chi Minh quoted the Declaration of Independence in his postcolonial struggle against France, and the civil rights movement inspired liberation movements across Africa and Asia.

And so the obvious question arises: Is America's true nature to be a predator or a promise? But that is dangerously simple. Let me suggest a different angle on America. Consider Richard Rodriguez's observation: Thomas Jefferson, that democrat, was a slaveholder. Thomas Jefferson, that slaveholder, was a democrat. The argument over the "essential" Jefferson, or the "essential" America, misses the point. America—like Jefferson, like each of us, like every country— is a trauma of contradictions. America can be a promise, a predator, or any number of a million other possibilities. None is inevitable. This, then, is the real question: Which America will be realized in the new millennium?

Calling all those who wish to make America a promise for all humanity. This is what we must do: Believe deeply, act boldly, begin now. Great nations are made of righteous strivings. Listen to the ancestors who worked to make America the promise a reality:

John Winthrop was the first governor of the Massachusetts Bay Colony, whose members set sail from England to build "a city set upon a hill" in America. He told his compatriots: "We must delight in each other, make others' conditions our own, rejoice together, mourn together, labor and suffer together, always having before our eyes our community as members of the same body."

Walt Whitman, who marveled at the diversity of voices in the world, held that all were from God and ached for connection between America and elsewhere:

the Christian priests at the altars of their churches
the Arab muezzin calling from the top of the mosque
the Hebrew reading his records and psalms
the Hindu teaching his favorite pupil
Each of us with his or her right upon the earth
Each of us here as divinely as any is here
What cities the light or warmth penetrate
I penetrate those cities myself
All islands to which birds wing their way I wing my way
  myself
I am a real Parisian
I am a habitant of Vienna, St. Petersburg, Berlin,
  Constantinople

James Baldwin, whose people came to America in chains but who insisted on being defined as a citizen with the right to shape America, said: "I am not a ward of America; I am one of the first Americans to arrive on these shores." Baldwin had a deep sense of America's problems and its potential to inspire freedom, equality, and brotherhood beyond its shores. He called on Americans to "end the racial nightmare, and achieve our country, and change the history of the world."

Jane Addams, who not only welcomed arriving souls to America but declared that the health of America's democracy depended on their participation, said: "We have learned to say that the good must be extended to all of society before it can be held secure by any one person or any one class; but we have not yet learned to add to that statement, that unless all [people] and all classes contribute to a good, we cannot even be sure it is worth having."

Martin Luther King Jr., who observed that since America's role had become global, so must its responsibilities, told us: "Through our scientific genius we have made of this world a neighborhood; now through our moral and spiritual development we must make of it a brotherhood." On a trip to India, the land of his hero, Mahatma Gandhi, King was shocked to see millions sleeping on the streets and going hungry every night. In a speech entitled "The American Dream," King declared: "The destiny of the United States is tied up with the destiny of India—with the destiny of every other nation. We spend more than a million dollars a day to store surplus food in this country. I know where we can store that food free of charge—in the wrinkled stomachs of the millions who go to bed hungry at night."

The songs of Woody Guthrie have American characters and scenery but a spirit that speaks to all humanity. I heard Woody's son Arlo Guthrie sing "This Land Is Your Land" at the Parliament of the World's Religions in Cape Town, South Africa. He told the crowd, "My daddy wrote this song for the whole world. When you hear the lines, 'From California to the New York Island,' know that you have to go the long way around."

To those working for America the promise, these past souls are wind at our back. They are angels of America, whispering in our ears, knocking at our doors, reminding us that we do not simply inherit the American tradition of righteousness; we must, as T. S. Eliot pointed out, work to deserve a place in it.

> *I've known rivers:*
> *Ancient, dusky rivers.*
> *My soul has grown deep like the rivers.*
> —Langston Hughes

America is a grand gathering of souls, the vast majority from elsewhere. And America is one of humanity's most ambitious experiments because it allows itself to be shaped by arriving souls. The American tradition of righteousness gives new life to arriving souls, and we contribute our stories to strengthen that tradition.

I am an American citizen with a Muslim soul. My soul carries a fourteen-hundred-year history of heroes, movements, and civilizations that sought to submit to the will of

Allah (the Arabic term for God). My soul hid in the cave with Prophet Muhammad during his journey from Mecca to Medina, protected from enemy search parties by Allah's gifts—the web of a spider, the branches of an acacia tree, the nest of a rock dove—scared but confident that his mission to bring peace and unity to the tribes of Arabia would be realized. After the death of the Prophet, my soul spread East and West, praying in the mosques and studying in the libraries of the great medieval Muslim cities of Baghdad, Cairo, and Cordoba. My soul whirled with Rumi, read Aristotle with Averroes, and traveled through Central Asia with Nasir Khusraw. Centuries later my soul was stirred to justice against colonial regimes in India and South Africa. It marched with Abdul Ghaffar Khan as he joined with Gandhi's *satyagraha* movement for Indian independence. It stood with Farid Esack, Ebrahim Moosa, and the Muslim Youth Movement in solidarity with black South Africans against the racist violence of apartheid.

The stories of my Muslim soul give the American tradition of righteousness new texture. I bring the story of Bilal, a slave in Muhammad's home city, Mecca. Prophet Muhammad's companions freed Bilal, and the Prophet elevated this former slave to a position of leadership within his community.

I bring the Qur'an's guidance on brotherhood: "O humankind, Allah has created you from male and female that you may come to know each other. Verily, the most honored of you in the sight of Allah is he who is the most righteous."

I bring the cosmic poetry of Rumi:

I am not from the East
or the West, not out of the ocean or up
from the ground
My place is placeless, a trace
of the traceless.
I belong to the beloved, have seen the two
worlds as one and that one call to and know

And, for this moment of possibility, I bring the story of the greater jihad. After victory in a battle during the early years of Islam, the Prophet declared that the Muslims were to move from the lesser jihad to the greater jihad. The lesser jihad was the battle against the external enemy. The greater jihad was the battle within, against their own lower selves.

America has been both promise and predator. Which will emerge in the new millennium? Will we achieve our country, build the city on the hill for all to see and help all humanity live the true American dream? Or will America's lower self—the imperialist predator drunk on greed, the vain bully content with being the lesser evil—creep to the surface?

There are people in power who seem intent on making America a predator. But they cannot silence the echoes of our tradition of righteousness, or smother the sparks of our contemporary movements for justice. America the promise is a possibility. We need to wage a greater jihad to make it a reality.

Anger and Its Effects on Us, and the World

THICH NHAT HANH

"If we have enough mindfulness and concentration, it can be easy for us to practice looking deeply into the nature of what is there, and to get insight. When you have insight, you can be liberated from your suffering. You have a path through, and you don't have to suffer much. . . . To me, the kingdom of God—the Pure Land of the Buddha— is not an invention of our thought, an abstract notion that is not real. It is available in the here and the now. If we are capable of establishing ourselves in the here and the now, we can touch the kingdom of God."

—Thich Nhat Hanh

Editors' note

The words of Thich Nhat Hanh, Buddhist monk and peace activist, have inspired millions of people around the world to the practices of mindfulness meditation: mindful breathing and mindful walking. The dharma talks, or teachings, that Thich Nhat Hanh gives at his retreat community at Plum Village in France, at his American dharma centers in Vermont and California, and at gatherings in cities worldwide all deliver the same message: anger is violence, but mindfulness will transform the seeds of anger into seeds of joy and compassion. The key to this Buddhist spiritual practice is diligence.

America's reputation as a hardworking—indeed diligent—nation is well earned. Every group of immigrants to arrive has been swept up into the hurry-and-worry of the American dream of success, but success does not lead to the kind of happiness that Thich Nhat Hanh speaks about. In fact, it may lead to anger, to selfishness, to suffering. In this excerpt from a dharma talk given recently in Providence, Rhode Island, Thich Nhat Hanh offers Americans the opportunity to help one another become truly present in the here and now. Then, according to the teachings of the Buddha, we will be in a position to get in touch with all the wonders of life. And we must ask ourselves, What difference could such a mindful attitude make in America's relationship to the community of the world?

Anger and Its Effects on Us, and the World
Thich Nhat Hanh

If you don't have enough mindfulness, you will be carried away by your anger. When anger manifests herself, your mind, your speech, and your action will be mobilized by her energy. This is because anger—her nature—is violence.

The willingness to punish, the willingness to bring harm to the other person, because we think that the other person is the source of our own suffering, or the other group of people are the source of our own suffering, comes from the energy of anger. With a practice—especially a practice of mindful breathing, mindful walking—we generate the energy of mindfulness that is needed to recognize every kind of mental formation that manifests in the upper level of our consciousness. If a wholesome, positive mental formation manifests like joy, or compassion, mindfulness is able to recognize that energy, and that joy can come to us very quickly. And when we hold that joy and compassion in us—it can grow—not only in the upper level of our consciousness but in the lower levels.

The seeds of joy and compassion—if you invite them very often, and if you know how to maintain them as long as possible—are able to grow. The same thing is true of our anger and our despair. If you allow your anger and despair to manifest, to open, and if you do not know how to help them, to reduce their importance, to bring relief to them, to look deeply into them in order to help them transform, they will grow day and night.

That is why we have to learn the art of taking care of mental formations. Diligence is one of the positive mental formations. Diligence means what? In a Buddhist context, it means several kinds of practice. The first kind of practice is this: If the negative mental formation has not manifested, then you try to keep it down there, by skillful means. Do not allow it to manifest. Second, if the negative mental formation has manifested, try your best to bring it back. There are many ways of doing so, and do not use violence. You recognize them, and you use skillful means to invite it to go back to sleep. One of the many methods is to invite the negative mental formation up, and then invite another positive mental formation—beauty and joy—up to neutralize it. You can help to return the first mental formation to its original form. There are many ways to do so, and we should be able to learn to do it.

The third aspect of the practice of diligence is this: If the positive mental formation has not had time to manifest, then try your best in order to help them to manifest. You can ask your friends, your brothers and sisters in the practice, to help you. You are his friend, you are her friend; you know the good things in her, and if you know how to speak about it, you will help each other.

In Plum Village, we call this the practice of selective watering. You don't water the negative seeds; you only try to water the positive seeds in you and in others. You should be able to tell him or her: "I vow not to water the negative seeds in you. I will be very careful. I will try my best not to water the seeds of anger, of irritation, of despair, of jealousy in you. I hope you will help me and will do the same. You know my weakness; therefore, please help me by only watering the positive seeds in me. Try your best not to water the negative seeds in me." If we do that, and we help each other in that way, we will suffer much less, and our joy and our happiness will increase every day.

We have fifty-one categories of seeds in us,[1] and we have to recognize that some of the seeds are very strong in us and in the other person. So, we have to help each other not to allow the negative seeds to manifest too often.

There are so many positive, wholesome mental formations in us, but we should remember at least three of them, and try to help them to grow in every moment of our life.

The first is mindfulness, the second is concentration, and the third is insight. If we have enough of the energy of mindfulness, and enough of the energy of concentration, we surely have insight.

To meditate means to look deeply into the nature of reality. Reality can be a flower, or a cloud, or a mental formation like anger or depression or compassion. Reality can be our despair. And if we have enough mindfulness and concentration, it can be easy for us to practice looking deeply into the nature of what is there, and to get insight. When you have insight, you can be liberated from your suffering. You have a path through, and you don't have to suffer much.

Mindfulness can be cultivated by a daily practice. When you prepare your breakfast, you may learn to prepare your breakfast in mindfulness. You become aware of every act—of your breathing, of your smiling. You can notice mindfulness all the way through, and making breakfast can become a joy, can become a meditation practice. You don't have to go to a meditation center. You can just stay in your kitchen.

When you open the water tap, allow the water to fall on your finger and bring your attention to it. The freshness of the water on your finger is very pleasant, and with a little bit of concentration and insight, you can see that the water has come from the top of the mountains; this water has been the snow, the ice, has been a cloud. It is so wonderful to be in touch with the cloud, the snow, the ice, and it has come to you.

Happiness is something that can be very simple. You enjoy deeply the contact with the water, but if you are in a hurry, you are being carried away by another mental formation: forgetfulness, the opposite of mindfulness. You are not aware of what you are doing, and therefore you do not enjoy what you are doing.

We have been running all our lives. Mindfulness helps us to establish ourselves in the here and the now. When you begin breathing in and breathing out in mindfulness, you bring your mind back to your body. When your mind and your body are together, you become truly present in the here and the now, and you are in a position to get in touch with all the wonders of life.

According to the teaching of the Buddha, life is only available in the present moment, and your only appointment with life is in that moment. If you miss that moment, you miss your appointment with life.

Therefore, mindful breathing or mindful walking

helps you to go back to the present moment. All of us know that the wonders of life are there somewhere, but there is some kind of obstacle that prevents us from getting in touch.

To me, the kingdom of God—the Pure Land of the Buddha—is not an invention of our thought, an abstract notion that is not real. It is available in the here and the now. If we are capable of establishing ourselves in the here and the now, we can touch the kingdom of God.

---

1. According to Buddhist psychology, our consciousness is divided into eight parts, including mind consciousness *(manovijñana)* and store consciousness *(alayavijñana)*. Store consciousness is described as a field in which every kind of seed can be planted—seeds of suffering, sorrow, fear, and anger, and seeds of happiness and hope. When these seeds sprout, they manifest in our mind consciousness, and when they do, they become stronger. There are fifty-one categories of these seeds.

Part 3

Making Change through Our Spiritual Communities

America as an
Interspiritual
Superpower:
A Vision to Be
Realized
WAYNE TEASDALE

"A broad, interspiritual American culture is being born and is becoming increasingly conscious, aware of a horizon of meaning and spiritual life that can overpower the predominant culture of entertainment, consumerism, and an essentially heartless capitalism. Under the surface of this society, with the intense meditative discipline being observed by several millions of spiritual seekers, a torrent of consciousness is rising in American humanity and other nations as well that will have its effect in time."

—**Wayne Teasdale**

Editors' note

Wayne Teasdale, lay Roman Catholic monk and student of Bede Griffiths, shows us a side to America that we don't often take time to notice. He identifies the leaven of "inter-spirituality" in ourselves and our communities and urges us to grow it. He defines interspirituality as "openness to other traditions of faith, wisdom, and spiritual life. Interspiritu-ality is also, more concretely, the willingness to explore these other traditions and to imbibe spiritual practices in these other systems of spirituality."

Teasdale is not as interested as some of the other con-tributors in debating the merits or demerits of American uses of power at home and abroad. He is reaching higher, so to speak, desiring that America become a more "noble kind of superpower, this light to the nations, and the worlds beyond." What could follow would be the changes that would affect all of our behaviors and actions, including a sense of solidarity with all beings, a deep humility, mature self-knowledge, and a commitment to compassionate service.

Teasdale's is a call to Americans to awaken to this potential within themselves. Like a prophet, he foretells the future:

> [Interspirituality] will have an influence on econom-ics, on capitalism, on the process of globalization, and on our corporate institutions by awakening heart in all of them, with integrity, as well as a social and ecolog-ical responsibility. Our foreign policy will be forged in a more enlightened place.

America as an Interspiritual Superpower:
A Vision to Be Realized
Wayne Teasdale

I t is not an exaggeration to say that in the long, troubled history of this fragile but exquisite planet there has not been a more inventive society than America. It is surely true that there are many societies with equal creativity, for instance, the ancient Greeks, the Arabs during the golden age of Islam, classical China, India, Japan, Germany, France, Spain, and Britain. Then there are the unique approaches to the natural world and culture found in numerous indigenous societies, notably the Australian Aborigines, Native Americans, and the countless tribes of Africa.

Creativity is a universal human attribute, and yet in the United States this precious trait has received a scope of activity that is virtually unlimited. In this sense, America can be regarded rightly as a multifaceted inventive genius, a practical intelligence that knows no bounds.

American preeminence can be seen in politics, economics, military power, law, governance, literature and entertainment, social consciousness and altruism, its eloquent espousal of human rights, and its deep-seated compassion when this people is in touch with its soul, its original source of inspiration, and the depth of its spiritual capacities. The other contributors to this volume have developed some of these other aspects of the American contribution to the world. It must also be mentioned how America has failed. The United States has not done much to close the gap between the haves and have-nots. Its foreign policy in recent years has lacked the maturity and selflessness one would expect of the only superpower. It continues to support an essentially heartless capitalism, the moral bankruptcy of which is clearly evident in the corporate scandals, the decay of our cities with respect to the urban poor, and the frightful exploitation of cheap labor with undocumented aliens in the United States, in Mexico, and elsewhere. An inhuman, unethical approach to vulnerable populations of employees is routinely practiced by many corporations without much integrity in their leadership. There is also the terrible failure of American culture in generating and disseminating our artificial, economically motivated culture through globalization, the similarly heartless process of extending American influence abroad. There is the huge problem of homelessness around the globe, with an estimated one billion persons living in the streets or in utter destitution—more than half a million (a conservative estimate) in the United States alone.

But these failures and successes are not what I will focus on in this essay. I wish to share a dream of America as an interspiritual superpower, a great society in which the acceptance of diversity and pluralism is innate to the psyche of this land, where it reaches a depth of integration that can be of benefit to the whole of humanity in this very dangerous period of history into which we have been thrust by tragic circumstances and by serious challenges requiring perspective and wisdom.

In what follows, I want to explore another avenue of greatness never mentioned in our society: the very real possibility and probability that America could emerge in time as a spiritual, or what I call an interspiritual, super-power. "Interspirituality" is a term I have coined to name and identify the phenomenon of our age of openness to other traditions of faith, wisdom, and spiritual life. Interspirituality is also, more concretely, the willingness to explore these other traditions and to imbibe spiritual practices in these other systems of spirituality. I have elaborated the meaning of this approach/phenomenon in both *The Mystic Heart* and *A Monk in the World*. First, it is necessary to consider some background.

A SOCIETY AT THE CROSSROADS

American culture in this period is spiritually illiterate, morally confused or ambiguous, psychologically dysfunctional, and addicted to violence, consumerism, and entertainment. It is true that most people in the United States are religious, or identify themselves as so, and all these people believe in God—some 97 percent—but only a small percentage of those actually understand that life is a spiritual process, a spiritual journey with a definite destination and purpose in mind.

Similarly, American culture is morally confused and steeped in ambiguity. It is confused about abortion, the death penalty, war, and the tolerance of all kinds and levels of violent behavior. In this, Hollywood is greatly to blame. It is responsible for this culture of violence to which we are subject because we live here. It feeds us a steady diet of violent films, videos, and TV series, and so maintains this cultural malaise of addiction to all sorts of violence. We accept this situation because of the spiritual illiteracy that exists at the basis of our world. It makes us ambiguous about these matters to which we are constantly exposed.

Spiritual illiteracy and moral confusion result in psychological dysfunction, affecting every aspect of our lives: our relationships in the family; our friendships; our work environment and how we relate to associates; our aspirations, ambitions, dreams, and fears; even our health. This psychological dysfunction has to do with ignorance, incapacity in our relationships, a lack of sufficient generosity, the desire for entertainment, and fixation on consumerism. It moves people to accept so much less than they can achieve in their spiritual lives by a deadening attachment to what is radically passing away. American culture is radically attached to the impermanent, and in a very real sense, September 11 was a lesson in this attachment and its ultimate futility.

It is not all negative, however, because there is in our society a prevailing, deeply rooted religious and spiritual freedom. It is profoundly guarded as a precious attainment of the American psyche. America has attracted all races, cultures, religions, and spiritualities, and we are the most ethnically, culturally, and religiously diverse society in the world. This is clearly the case in our major cities of Chicago, New York City, Los Angeles, and Seattle.

America has welcomed all the religions of the world. It is no longer dominated by Protestants, Catholics, and Jews, since now Hindus, Buddhists, Muslims, Jains, and Sikhs exist here in great numbers. There are more Muslims— some seven million of them in the United States—than Episcopalians. Every faith and form of spirituality is here, and since the 1960s, truly gifted spiritual teachers and masters are here, operating centers, and with large numbers of devotees following them. Many indigenous traditions are also represented, including Native American faiths and Latin American shamans, with their natural mysticism. Maharishi Mahesh Yogi, the transcendental meditation master; Swami Satchidananda, founder of the Integral Yoga Institutes; Zen roshis; Tibetan rinpoches; Kabbalistic and Hasidic teachers; Thomas Merton and Thomas Keating, Trappist spiritual masters; Pir Vilayat Inayat Khan and his successor and son, Pir Zia, the Sufi inspiring lights; Lama Palden Drolma, a woman who is a Tibetan Buddhist teacher—all of these figures and countless others are part of a growing movement to genuine and mature spirituality. All these streams of mystical wisdom are available here and are mingling in the great American spiritual culture. Their existence in America helps raise the level of awareness of many people, and these leaders are passing on their insights, their methods of prayer and contemplation and meditation with its accompanying psychology, and their insights into cultivating community as a foundation for transformation of more and more people.

When the interfaith movement is added to these streams of mystical wisdom, there is a possibility for a huge breakthrough in American culture, setting the stage for something never seen before in our hemisphere: the emergence of a spiritual superpower, reminiscent of the golden age of India's mystical, contemplative civilization. This extraordinary emergent reality is the result of a growing cultural, religious, intellectual, artistic, and spiritual ferment stimulated by the incredible intensification of diversity in one area of the world, and manifesting itself on such a high level of articulation and maturity.

This ferment is also an interlocking of capacities that, as they interact, create other capacities that generate conditions for new cultural forms. A broad, interspiritual American culture is being born and is becoming increasingly conscious of a horizon of meaning and spiritual life that can overpower the predominant culture of entertainment, consumerism, and an essentially heartless capitalism. Under the surface of this society, with the intense meditative discipline being observed by several millions of spiritual seekers, a torrent of consciousness is rising in American humanity and in other nations as well that will have its effect in time.

THE INTERFAITH MOVEMENT, COMMUNITY, AND THE BIRTH OF INTERSPIRITUALITY

The concentration of such an intensification of spiritual genius in all its cultural expressions from all the great world religions, spiritualities, and systems of mystical wisdom has been made possible by the blossoming of the interreligious, or interfaith, movement with its opportunities for substantial encounter, mutual exchange, mystical irradiation, and cross-fertilization of insight, perception, and dialectical possibilities for newer understandings of what is real and true, with attendant strategies for approaching the Divine, the Absolute.

This interfaith movement in the modern age began in September 1893 in Chicago during the World's Parliament of the Religions, which brought the venerable faith traditions together for the first time in historical memory for seventeen days as part of the World's Colombian Exposition, the World's Fair. From this event, Hinduism, Buddhism, Jainism, and Shinto were introduced into American culture, and the West more generally, but it was not until further historical occurrences that something jelled on a deeper level of development, sparking the possibility of an interspiritual awakening. These occurrences were the Second Vatican Council (1962–1965) and the Parliament of the World's Religions in Chicago, August 28 to September 5, 1993. Both these events and processes have contributed to where we are today. Vatican II greatly advanced interreligious dialogue and encounter by opening the Roman Catholic Church to dialogue with, and respect for, the other traditions. The Roman Catholic Church has really been a leader in interfaith conversation and collaboration. The Church's action, especially in the recognition of truth and moral values in the other religions announced in the conciliar document *Nostra Aetate*, set the stage for vigorous and persistent activity of an interreligious nature. Roman Catholics have been in the forefront of this work since its inception with the teaching of the council, and monastics have contributed enormously to the contemplative dimension of interfaith exchange.

The second most important event has been the 1993 Parliament of the World's Religions, the centennial celebration of the historically significant Chicago happening. This great event, like Vatican II, was a world historical process that allowed the insight of the moment to reach a culmination in community as the new paradigm, or model, of how the religions, in their members, relate to one another. I foresaw and then witnessed this reality of community come into being during the 1993 Parliament. It was a miracle of human interaction, of cross-religious experience, almost a second Pentecost.

The birth of community and its cultivation in the context of live-in opportunities in the interfaith matrix—especially in the intermonastic exchange, the increase in dialogical activities, and the growth of understanding—have contributed to the phenomenon of interspirituality. Let me characterize the reality of the interspiritual concept/experience, an ever-expanding radius of light from all the spiritual paths in each of the traditions.

Interspirituality arises where the mystical life fruitfully manifests itself in a person's experience, consciousness, and actions. All three are in contact with the Divine, the Absolute, God, Spirit, infinite consciousness, and are inspired. The mystical life, the spiritual journey, the evolution of the person brings that one to inner freedom, as a gift of knowing the Divine, being one with it, and the possibility—indeed longing—to explore and know the depth of mystical wisdom in all other traditions, particularly in ways relevant for, or related to, what the mystic, the person, intensely knows in a contemplative manner. Interspiritual wisdom dawns when a person has the freedom, the generosity, and the capacity to explore, delve into, and inwardly come to know the other traditions in a mystical sense.

America needs to awaken to this vision of knowing, because its vocation in this age so fraught with danger, darkness, and uncertainty is to shed the light of interspiritual wisdom in a world flirting with catastrophe. American culture, as a basic presupposition of its truth, life, and dynamic of civilization, is totally committed to diversity of views, faiths, spiritualities. And so, quite organically, naturally, and intrinsically required of American culture by its nature is that it be interspiritual—that is, open to and nourished by the spiritual treasures of all the world's venerable faiths.

America can be this noble kind of superpower, this light to the nations and to the worlds beyond. It can cultivate this intermystical openness that is what interspirituality is in its ultimate sense: a dynamic, creative perception of the wisdom in all traditions and ways of knowing, including science, creativity, music, poetry, art, and all human experience, uniting it in itself by integrating it, knowing it in the integration, and applying it to its culture, life, and society in all its modes of presence and activity. America can be all this because it has the capacity, nurtured by centuries, to accept not only the diversity of peoples and cultures here on these shores but the equality of these views, approaches to ultimate reality, a basic generosity, a spaciousness of being that allows it to welcome and embrace the great plurality, the bewildering and endlessly fascinating differences between and among persons. I have no doubt that this is the path of greatness for America now and in the future. In this way it will become inevitably an interspiritual superpower, like India in its day for so many millennia.

American spirituality, as becoming more and more interspiritual and intermystical, is a universal spirituality that is eminently practical in nine ways and, through these ways, becomes immensely transformative of the individual, the community, and the world. Interspirituality finds these nine elements in the mature expressions of spirituality in every tradition—that is, in their saints or mystics. These include (1) an actualized moral capacity; (2) a sense of solidarity and interdependence with all beings; (3) deep nonviolence; (4) humility of heart; (5) a spiritual practice; (6) mature self-knowledge; (7) simplicity of life; (8) love in action, or compassionate service; and (9) prophetic voice, or witness, and action.

The first way, or element, is moral consciousness, having an actualized moral life: that one is naturally moral. It has become second nature to the person. That's the foundation of the spiritual life, the path, the evolution of one's development. Second, the enlightened man or woman knows of his or her interdependence and joyful solidarity with all living beings in all worlds. Because of this, third, there is an innate commitment to nonharming of all beings with whom we come in contact, since we are all interconnected, and everything we do affects everyone and everything else. Fourth, it is humility of heart that knows, sees, acts aright in each situation. Humility of heart is honesty about yourself, who you are, and the integrity you have. Humility is a nonmanipulative relationship toward everyone, everything, and reality itself. One doesn't impose on or manipulate others but respects their inherent right to be, and to be respected. The fifth way or element of spirituality and interspirituality is spiritual practice, the utter necessity for it. It is primarily through a spiritual practice, the central commitment to a method of prayer, that the person pursues the spiritual life, in real dedication of praxis, whether in meditation, verbal prayer, singing, chanting, dancing, or giving adoration to the Divine. These and many other forms of spiritual practice become the ground of real inner and outer growth, especially when there is genuine transformation (which will be discussed), and they are the basis of great breakthroughs in the spiritual life.

The sixth is related to the fifth, in that self-knowledge often results from, and is the fruit of, prayer, meditation, or whatever form spiritual practice takes in the committed activity of the person. This self-knowledge is a precious gift from prayer, part of its fruit in knowledge of ourselves, our nature, and deeper motivations—motivations often hidden from view in the unconscious life of the person.

When we reach the seventh element or way of a universal spirituality, an intermystical spiritual path, we are in the clear understanding of the need for simplicity of life, which requires a more simple lifestyle. The aspect of spiritual life, of a viable American spirituality, connects us with nature and all beings. It makes it possible for us to simplify our needs so the planet, the natural world, is not harmed by our presence but greatly enhanced. It opens us to all others, especially the poor, because there are no material concerns that keep us apart. Being simple, we are open to the vulnerable, the poor, the marginalized of the world. It then makes us docile and receptive to the Divine.

Then comes the eighth element, or way of love in action, selfless service, or compassionate action. This capacity for love, kindness, compassion, even sensitivity is related to all the other elements and, in many ways, is the fruit of them in relation to all others. Spirituality is not genuine if it isn't engaged with the world—that is, with others. This attitude, activity, and being concretizes our spirituality; it makes it authentic, or real. It is this capacity that constitutes us most like God.

Closely related to the eighth element in its active orientation is the ninth and final element of American spirituality, as a viable interspirituality, and that is prophetic voice, witness, and action where warranted. Part of being an engaged spirituality is a concern with justice, with social and environmental responsibility, with the struggle for peace and the promotion of justice in the search for common ground and harmony. The enlightened individual will stick his or her neck out for the sake of justice, for others— that is, will take risks in order to help the vulnerable, marginalized, and ignored of society. A spirituality not so engaged is poor indeed. American spirituality is always so engaged when it arrives at maturity and greatness.

This spirituality, as a whole, is marked by this attitude and practice of engagement with others, with the world. Furthermore, it is holistic; it integrates the body, soul, and mind, or spirit, and it unites the conscious with the unconscious, and them to the superconsciousness. Finally, this spirituality is integral because it seeks to relate faith, mysticism, contemplation, science, and creativity—that is, unite all avenues of knowing.

The effect of this spirituality on the person is profound transformation, a substantial change from one state of awareness to another. This awareness takes in all the faculties of the person. One's understanding, character, will, emotions, imagination, memory, and behavior are all positively affected. Space does not permit me to detail this point by way of elaborating the impact on each faculty.

It can be said that when the American people and their culture awaken to the extent envisioned above, and our nation assumes the mantle of an interspiritual superpower, there will no doubt be constructive effects on our thinking as a nation and as persons. It will have an influence on economics, on capitalism, on the process of globalization, and on our corporate institutions by awakening heart in all of them, with integrity, as well as a social and ecological responsibility. Our foreign policy will be forged in a more enlightened place, with a more compassionate commitment to nonviolence, justice, genuine peace, and the disciplined pursuit of spirituality, mystical life, and the spiritual journey. Our culture would radiate acceptance of everyone and everything. There would be an emphasis on generosity, on sharing, which generates community everywhere, while our educational system would serve our ultimate development in our individual paths, all leading to a greater appreciation of our engagement with the mystery of otherness here and abroad.

American Empire and the War against Evil

ROSEMARY RADFORD RUETHER

"Above all [this imperial agenda] must be questioned for its idolatrous moral absolutism, for its claims to represent good against evil, God against the Devil, resisting any self-critique of its own power. Not only critics from the Muslim world and the third world, but also our European allies, are deeply offended by this direction of American power. . . . We need a new generation of prophets."

—Rosemary Radford Ruether

Editors' note

An indispensable tradition of the American experience has been the recurring voices of "prophetic critique" that point out our failures and call us back to renewed faithfulness to principles of "liberty and justice for all." Ecofeminist and Christian theologian Rosemary Radford Ruether fills such a role admirably in her forthright discussion of what's wrong with America's present drive toward imperialism. Why have the American people permitted militarism and an apparent attempt at world domination to take over our national politics, our economy, and indeed our souls? When will the prophets arise to steer us away from this destructive, immoral course?

Ruether lays out her plainly worded view that America, once meant to be a beacon of light for all humanity, has over the centuries allowed imperialist desires and self-interest to distort the righteousness of the American vision into a warped justification for world hegemonic power. Dangerous in its "idolatrous moral absolutism," America as superpower has set itself up to represent good against evil, God against the Devil. What will it take to awaken the prophets?

American Empire and
the War against Evil
Rosemary Radford Ruether

The United States has emerged as the greatest super-power in human history. Its political, economic, military, and cultural power reaches more parts of the entire globe than any previous empire. The Roman empire, the Chinese empire, the Islamic empire at their heights of power were parochial compared with the global reach of the United States. The critical question that confronts Americans and the peoples of the rest of the nations of the planet is how benign or destructive is this massive American power.

The United States has long entertained a sense of itself as unique and divinely chosen to be a model for the rest of the world. Our Puritan ancestors in the Massachusetts Bay Colony spoke of their settlement as a "city on a hill," called to be a beacon of light for all humanity. Nineteenth-century expansionists in the United States claimed that we had a "manifest destiny" to spread across the continent and into the Caribbean and Pacific islands, exhibiting to the world the superiority of our civic virtue and democratic institutions.

This ideology of American goodness and greatness, however, has generally been countered by voices of prophetic critique that pointed out our glaring failures and called us to repentance and renewed fidelity to the principles of "liberty and justice for all" as the heart of our civic creed. John Winthrop in 1630 warned that we could become cursed rather than blessed if we "played falsely with our God" and failed to exemplify the virtues to which we pretended.[1] Martin Luther King Jr. confronted us with the sorry history of slavery and racism and exhorted us to realize an American dream betrayed to our African American populace.

Having first emancipated itself from the British Empire in the late eighteenth century, the United States began to follow in the footsteps of that empire in the nineteenth century. With the Monroe Doctrine we staked our claims to rival British power in the Americas. After buying up or conquering French and Mexican territories within the continental United States, we put our feet on the path of empire with the Spanish-American War in 1898. In the first half of the twentieth century, repeated military interventions in Caribbean and Central American nations, such as Haiti, the Dominican Republic, and Nicaragua, showed our determination to prevent any independent path of political or economic development in what we defined as our backyard. In the second half of the twentieth century, this interventionism would become global, with major wars and coups in Korea, Vietnam, Guatemala, Nicaragua, Chile, and elsewhere, wrapped in the flag of anticommunism.

The end of World War II saw the collapse of the colonial empires of Britain, Holland, and France as these nations were forced to rebuild national economies shattered by the war. The United States, as the nation whose own national economy has been unscathed by the war, emerged as the defender of the Western capitalist world against the rival Communist bloc. This rivalry was defined not simply as political and economic but as ideological and theological. The term "godless communism" turned this power struggle into one of good against evil, God against godlessness. America defined itself as God's representative to defend a divinely blessed "way of life" and to extend it to the rest of the world against its diabolical enemies.

From the 1950s through the 1980s this American hegemonic power was seen as relatively benign by our European allies and by those elites around the world who benefited from our power. Deep anti-Americanism surfaced among those who aspired to "national liberation" from the American-led neocolonialism. But efforts to shake free of this power and to foster alternative paths to development were undermined and defeated by a combination of economic strangulation through the world financial institutions, embargo by the United States, and either direct or surrogate military intervention.

All of these methods were brought to bear to destroy the Sandinista revolution in Nicaragua in the 1980s, rendering this tiny nation more impoverished than before. As one American supporter of the revolution put it to me in Managua, "They had to destroy the threat of a good example," that is, the danger that an alternative way of development through democratic socialism might actually work to improve people's lives.

Although the Soviet Union was defined as our bête noire, its military power, economic aid, and ideological influence operated to create a certain global balance of power in the 1960s to the 1980s. The United States developed strategies of multilateral cooperation with our allies, collaboration in international treaties, and forms of assistance designed to show that the capitalist mode of development was superior to that of socialism, even while doing everything possible to prevent actual successes of the socialist path. In the late 1980s, however, it became evident that the Soviet Union was about to collapse and break up into its constituent nations. The USSR was economically exhausted by a $300 billion military budget that rivaled that of the United States but constituted 12 percent of its gross national product, in contrast to 6 percent of the gross national product of the United States. It could no longer hold together an alliance and form of government that had become distasteful to most of its people.

With the collapse of the Soviet Union, United States hegemonic militarism faced a crisis of legitimacy. Without communism as its enemy, its vast military budget and role as policeman of the world was in danger of losing its rationale. Many Americans began to speak of a peace dividend, anticipating a scaling-back of the huge Cold War military budget by half. They hoped to free large sums to rebuild the infrastructure of United States society such as roads and bridges, to refund schools, and to rethink matters such as national health insurance. Alarmed by such talk, the Pentagon began to cast its eyes across the globe for new enemies. It defined a military strategy as one that must be ready to fight "two wars at once" and lumped together remaining pockets of communism with militant Muslim nations as the enemies. In a precursor of George W. Bush's "axis of evil," it listed Cuba, North Korea, Libya, Iraq, and Iran among countries we must be ready to fight.

A new alliance of the Christian right, with its wars on gays, feminists, and reproductive rights, with national security and free trade neoconservatives who believed in American military and economic supremacy, had emerged in the Reagan years. This alliance seemed to be somewhat in retreat with the 1992 victory of Bill Clinton, who sought to capture a middle ground of American politics that included moderate concern for social welfare at home and humanitarianism abroad. But the weakness of this centrist vision, as well as his personal peccadilloes, laid the ground for a new victory of the alliance between Christian fundamentalists and proponents of national security, with the nonelection of George W. Bush in 2000.

The hard-right ideologues of this Bush "team," such as Richard Cheney, Donald Rumsfeld, and Paul Wolfowitz, had already laid the ideological ground in the mid-1990s for a different vision of the American future. With no international rival for hegemonic power, they believed that the way was clear for the United States to seize control of the world, eliminating not only any actual rivals but any potential rivals to American power. This new imperial dream would demand not a scaling-down but a vast increase of the American military budget, dwarfing the military budgets of the rest of the nations of the world. America was to have absolute military predominance, both to intervene militarily in any nation that threatened it, even before any attack had actually been mounted, and also to defend itself against any missiles that might be directed at our national territory.

With absolute military predominance, multilateral alliances, such as collaboration in curbing civil wars abroad, healing diseases, and preventing environmental degradation, could be discarded as not serving our "national interest." In the 1990s this took the form of a concerted attack on "big government," both federal government projects that nationalized funding and standards of social welfare and also the United Nations as a potential "world government" that might lessen the absolute sovereignty of the United States. Any kind of international law against violations of human rights that might possibly be applied to our personnel or our allies, such as Israel's Sharon or Chile's Pinochet, was seen as an intolerable affront to our national autonomy.

When George W. Bush came to power in 2001, he quickly showed his alignment with this program of unilateral and militaristic American power. In rapid succession, he curbed American contributions to international family planning, rejected American participation in the Kyoto climate treaty, dismantled international arms control treaties, and rejected the jurisdiction of the World Court for any crimes that might involve the United States. But this policy direction gained a new rationale with the terrorist attacks on the two major symbols of American military and economic power, the Pentagon and the World Trade Center, on September 11, 2001.

Tragic as this attack was for its victims, it was a bonanza for the Bush administration. September 11 gave the Bush administration the new global enemy it needed to justify its global imperial strategy. "Terrorism" became the new incarnation of evil. The fight against terrorism was defined not as a collaborative effort to defend all victimized nations against nonstate violence, but rather as a world war without end to be fought with the armaments of the most advanced military technology, including nuclear weapons. This was to be directed not only against the small enclaves of terrorists but against the nations that "harbored them."

Designating its global imperial strategy as a war against terrorism ensured the Bush regime of both a bipartisan consensus and popular support, while denouncing any critics of these policies as incipient traitors and collaborators with terrorists. With such a war against terrorism projected as virtually endless, the far-right ideologues sought to make their power permanent and irreversible in the United States and across the world. Thus, it is no surprise that, having pushed over the Taliban regime that supported the Al Qaeda network in Afghanistan (without apprehending its leaders), the Bush administration quickly set its sights on a larger goal, namely Iraq.

Iraq is the major target for American supremacists for two reasons: for its vast supplies of oil and because it represents unfinished business from the Gulf War of 1990. This is not a matter of a father-son psychological rivalry between Bush senior and Bush junior. Rather, Iraq represents a challenge to the imperial hegemony of the United States and its client state, Israel, over the Middle East. Even though his famous "weapons of mass destruction" have become elusive, Saddam Hussein represents an aspiration to leadership in the Arab world. Though his country is weakened and impoverished under international sanctions, he continues to thumb his nose at American demands for control. To smash his remaining power and to reshape this nation to our imperial demands has become a main demand of both ideological and military-economic supremacists in the United States.

But the designs of world hegemonic power that underlie this crusade against Iraq must be, more than ever, clothed in the vestments of absolute moral righteousness. Saddam Hussein must be depicted as a diabolic plotter who threatens the national security of the United States and the whole world. Even though his military budget is a pittance compared with that of the United States ($1.4 billion versus more than $400 billion), his weapons must be seen as threatening to overwhelm those of the United States. His evil treatment of his own people and his neighbors is undoubtedly worthy of criticism, but the rhetoric used to denounce these evils conceals the fact that most of these crimes were committed when he was an ally of the United States and with the connivance of the very critics who now attack him. The plans for war against Iraq are depicted as one more episode in an apocalyptic drama of good against evil, the angels of Light against the forces of Darkness, America as God's chosen people against God's enemies.

What are we to say about the emergence of America as a superpower in the first decade of the twenty-first century? Is it a force primarily for human good or for evil? It is my belief that the direction charted by the Bush administration to direct American power toward global empire is a disaster both for the world and for the American people itself. It means dismantling many of the fragile structures of international cooperation designed to curb militarism and to foster social welfare, environmental health, and peace. It will further inflame hatred of the United States, both in the Islamic world and in much of the "third world," and will also antagonize many in Europe.

This imperial agenda will also further distort the U.S. economy, delaying any reinvestment in needed infrastructure, education, health, and social welfare. The whole world, and finally ourselves, will be impoverished, both morally and economically, by this wrongheaded drive for imperial power. Above all, it must be questioned for its idolatrous moral absolutism, for its claims to represent good against evil, God against the Devil, resisting any self-critique of its own power. Not only critics from the Muslim world and the third world, but also our European allies, are deeply offended by this direction of American power.

American people themselves must challenge a domestic and foreign policy that guts our own traditions of democracy, human rights, and prophetic self-critique. We need a new generation of prophets to arise to denounce the misuse of American might for blatant power-mongering and self-enrichment of the superrich. Even more, we need new prophets who will redefine how America can become, once again, one nation among others in a world community that seeks "liberty and justice for all."

---

1. For this citation of Winthrop, as well as the general inspiration of this article, see Tom Barry,"El complejo de poder: se acabo 'el gringo bueno'" in *Envio: Revista Mensual de la Universidad Centroamericana*, November 2002 (no. 248), 45–50.

Congregation versus Superpower: The Inner Work for Peace in the Local Community of Faith

REV. WILLIAM McD. TULLY

"Though Christianity began as, and has often been, the cradle of prophetic pacifism, it's very tough to practice a radically consistent nonviolence, at least if you are honest enough to begin with yourself. And it seems to me that any hope religious types have in influencing our role as superpower will founder if we're perceived to be hypocritical."

—Rev. William McD. Tully

Editors' note

One of the most basic spiritual questions in the world is: Where do you live? How we interpret our place in the world tells volumes about the rest of our spiritual or religious beliefs. Are you at home on this planet? Are you yearning for something beyond? Are you separated from others, from the Divine—or are you somehow close?

Rev. Bill Tully explains that conservative Christians have always had good theological reasons for believing that the use of violence was sometimes necessary. Conservative Christians do not see themselves as entirely "of this world." As John Wilson wrote in his contribution to this book, many believe in a sort of "dual citizenship."

Tully quotes the sixteenth-century Swiss Protestant reformer John Calvin: "How foolish is the conceit of those, who seek to take away the use of the sword, on account of the Gospel. We might indeed do without the sword, were we angels in this world; but the number of the godly, as I have already said, is small; it is therefore necessary that the rest of the people should be restrained by a strong bridle."

But that is not nearly enough, according to Tully. Spiritual people understand that "inner work" informs the rest of life. Tully is committed to building what Christian theology calls an "earthly kingdom," where peace and generosity reign. This is the purpose of religious communities such as Tully's St. Bartholomew's Episcopal Church in Manhattan. He urges that both a "use of the sword"—justified by conservatives—and old-fashioned liberal optimism and passion are not enough; change within always precedes change without.

Congregation versus Superpower: The Inner Work for Peace in the Local Community of Faith
Rev. William McD. Tully

I n a society often consumed with the merely urgent, America's local religious congregations are seedbeds of reflection on the truly important things in life. That will surprise cynics, both religious and secular, who see churches, synagogues, mosques, or temples as little more than cells of obedience, rote, and ritual.

The power of religion in local community is needed as never before, now that history has left the United States as the world's lone superpower. Our nation's soul and spirit are rooted in the souls of people. People do their soul work with others who are touched by the traditions and scriptures of those who know the positive uses, and the temptations, of power.

Local religious life—by most estimates lived in about 350,000 congregations of all kinds—is lively and varied and bears little relationship to media preoccupation with institutional decline, televangelism, or abusive behavior by clergy. Down here, where we live our faith, we also think, pray, meditate, and experiment with the life-and-death questions.

My own congregation is one example. Outwardly it defies the older stereotype of the village church and the newer one of the shiny, suburban spiritual megamall. It lives in (and barely pays for) a grand landmark structure on Park Avenue, deep in a canyon of skyscrapers housing many of America's Fortune 500 companies. Its carriage-trade congregants have gone the way of social change. But it beats with the heart of a great city, and it is becoming as diverse—economically and socially, racially and theologically—as its city. It prays and sings, educates and cares for its members. It seeks to be a voice of faith in a noisy culture. It feeds and shelters the poor (yes, on Park Avenue) every day and night of the year. Through it all, and like so many of its spiritual peers, our congregation is a place of meaning for its members.

And when the Bush administration suddenly, or so it seemed to many, defined our post–September 11 national security in terms of Iraqi honesty about its weapons of mass destruction, my parishioners responded as if stuck with a political and ethical needle they hadn't felt in a generation.

I can't remember a time when more people virtually ordered up a sermon. The hunger for meaning was palpable.

Sometimes the order came as a question: "What does the church think about war in Iraq?" Sometimes it was a plea: "Tell us what we can do. Should we stand by helplessly as our nation slides into another war?" Sometimes the order took a position: "How can you let the president get away with it, taking us along a dangerous path when he hasn't made his case?" Or, this from one of our many members who are not American citizens: "I love your country, but do you know that with your power and arrogance you, who got our sympathy when you suffered from terror a year ago, are now seen as an arrogant bully in danger of becoming an international outlaw?" Many of our more conservative members seemed rattled, too. One wondered plaintively whether there was anyone in the (larger) church anywhere who cared about our commander-in-chief, our troops, or our security.

When I had gathered my thoughts and said my prayers and had come, with fear and trembling, to the moment of preaching the requested sermon, I began this way: "Some of you have spoken impatiently and challenged me to give voice to what you believe is obvious as a Christian position and is required of one who presumes to take that position in preaching and teaching. Not to be flip, but be careful what you ask or pray for. And be cautious in your assumptions."

I reasoned that the last thing needed by thoughtful, pained, and open-minded believers and citizens was to have their anxieties magnified or their prejudices confirmed. Historically, Christians have been most effective not when they are most numerous or powerful but when they are a small, activist leaven in the lump.

More than on most Sundays, my aim was specifically to teach. I stand in a tradition that does not believe the church is a hierarchy, where the pulpit is the place to instruct people on what to think and do. Instead, we seek to teach ourselves how to think and therefore to decide what to do. I set out to equip my parishioners with the tools of their tradition for, to use Harry Emerson Fosdick's hymnic words, "the facing of this hour." In this I hoped to avoid the tiresome result C. S. Lewis referred to when he said that when preachers write prayers about or take positions on national and international politics, they usually reveal little more than which newspapers are read in the rectory.

I predicted at the outset that a number of my listeners would be disappointed. If I had heard them correctly, they wanted something from me that I couldn't necessarily give— confirmation of their opinions about their government and their nation's role and position in the world. But it was those in particular I had in mind. I reminded them that nearly every Sunday before the sermon I invited them to pray that God would "take our minds and think through them."

The news that week provided my nonbiblical text: the Congress of the United States had voted strongly to give President Bush authority to wage war preemptively in Iraq. I noted two apparently agreed-upon realities in this context. One, the polls show that a majority of Americans have doubts about the wisdom of this course of action. And two, an even greater majority agree that Saddam Hussein is, as Mr. Bush said, "a homicidal dictator," with a bloody history of aggression against his own people and his neighbors, and that he possesses weapons of mass destruction.

Christianity has had a divided, almost schizophrenic relationship with state authority. Beginning as an often-despised proletarian and mostly pacifist sect, the church rather suddenly became the religion of empire. The motive for conversion was closely related to imperial military victory. Now that America is the lone superpower in the world, we may have come uncomfortably full circle—Pax Romana to Pax Americana. I felt bound to say that "whatever the disappointments you and I feel in the administration and the political parties, this set of circumstances makes it tough to be a leader. We may rail at them over the op-ed page and our morning coffee, but if we mean what we say in our worship today, we should also pray for them." Looking back on it, I would want to add "and pray for ourselves." It is unbecoming, too easy, and ultimately useless to say "them" as if our leaders were not in some true sense "us."

And we can add to the context the messy reality of the Christian and wider religious community in this nation. No free nation—and we're the freest on the planet—pays as much attention to its religious life as we do. But not only are we not a theocracy; our freedom extends to and down within our churches, synagogues, mosques, and temples. Some prominent preachers echo the president's position. The majority of the Christian churches—the Roman Catholic bishops, the mainstream Protestant judicatories, most of the academic establishment in Christianity, and a substantial part of the Jewish community—have moderate to severe reservations about this national policy. And mostly they are saying, "A pox on both your houses." They are not impressed with the political opposition, and they worry, to say the least, about what the majority has declared is to be the American position.

Those in favor of the course Mr. Bush has championed and has skillfully gotten the Congress to endorse rely on a long tradition, based on biblical sources, that the world and the church are not contiguous. Listen to the great Protestant reformer John Calvin. His has become the honored position in the evangelical community and among many (and I use this carefully and in quotes) "conservative Christians."

> So far as any one embraces the doctrine of the Gospel, so far he becomes gentle and seeks to do good to his neighbors. But as we as yet carry about us the relics of sin in our flesh, and as our knowledge of the Gospel is not yet perfect, it is no wonder, that not one of us has hitherto wholly laid aside the depraved and sinful affections of his flesh. It is also easy hence to see, how foolish is the conceit of those, who seek to take away the use of the sword,

on account of the Gospel. We might indeed do without the sword, were we angels in this world; but the number of the godly, as I have already said, is small; it is therefore necessary that the rest of the people should be restrained by a strong bridle; for the children of God are found mixed together, either with cruel monsters or with wolves and rapacious men. Some are indeed openly rebellious, others are hypocrites. The use of the sword will therefore continue to the end of the world.[1]

There's some hard reality in that position. I wanted my congregation to hear it and squirm a little: "Think about it close to home. Who among us would not use force to protect our children and others in our household—or even in a flash to guard our property? And New Yorkers know well that we authorize the use of force by our civil police. We couldn't live without them and the force we allow them, though we know how delicate the balance is and how often that force has been abused."

In other words, though Christianity began as, and has often been, the cradle of prophetic pacifism, it's very tough to practice a radically consistent nonviolence—at least if you are honest enough to begin with yourself. And it seems to me that any hope religious types have in influencing our role as superpower will founder if we're perceived to be hypocritical.

Evangelicals, most of whom are politically conservative, may have the upper hand at this moment. Once radically averse to politics, conservative American Christians and other religionists have eclipsed the moderate to liberal majority in political influence. Often their position sounds warmly patriotic in its transparency and clarity.

The "mainline" Christian position is by nature subtle and nuanced. It takes longer to explain, and it admits the risk of practicing a patriotism closer to a lover's quarrel than blind loyalty.

This is the tradition in Christian thought that suggests a way to live that takes with utmost seriousness the messy involvement of God in history—collected, debated, refined, and applied in the Bible. It's a tradition America the superpower needs more than ever. And if this tradition of ethical subtlety is to have public influence, it must be rooted in teaching and reflection in the pews of the American congregations that are perhaps the new "silent majority."

When I assert that this ethical tradition is found in the Bible, I mean the broad message of the Bible, not a selection of proof texts. A Washington friend and mentor of mine, Philip Wogaman, has helped me and others see this in a comprehensive way. He has taught generations of students at Wesley Seminary and has preached to a troubled presidency at Foundry Methodist Church, so he has tested what he has believed and taught.

This is the teaching I wish were as familiar on Capitol Hill as the slogans both sides lob at each other. Just once, I wish for a public figure with the sure heart and nimble mind to spin out (maybe even on PBS's *NewsHour*) a genuine Christian ethic that people could understand, who would admit to using it to inform his or her own conscience. It's the teaching I commend to my parishioners. I hope they will claim it and, at the least, use it when analyzing what the president and Congress and their favorite or least favorite op-ed writers are saying.

In Wogaman's crisp formulation, there are basic moral presumptions all Christians share, no matter what their denomination or politics. He names four positive presumptions and two negative ones. He takes them from a broad reading of scripture and thousands of years of testing and trying in ancient Israel and in the dispersed Christian communities.

Christians positively presume:

- The goodness of the created order
- The value of human life
- The unity of the human family in God
- The equality of persons before God

Christians negatively presume:

- Human finitude, which limits our perception of the good
- Human sinfulness, which predisposes us to act in our own self-interest

These moral presumptions become an ethical template, a way of saying that Christians cannot and should not make decisions in a vacuum. We have a tradition. It has content. God has acted in history, and for us supremely through the person and historical event that is Jesus of Nazareth. When we call Jesus the Christ, we mean the one "anointed" by God to bring a new reality.

However open-minded we are, we must admit that we do not start with a blank slate. We bring a tilt to every argument. Or, if you have ever engaged in formal debate, the burden of proof in this moment is on those who would make war. Quite simply, the tilt in Christianity is always toward peace.

On that Sunday I delivered the ordered-up sermon, I reminded myself and my listeners that "sophisticated New York Episcopalians, who mostly seem to have a soft preference for liberalism, should take stock of the force of their tradition. Some of us often sound as militantly presumptuous of our own political and social biases as those fellow Americans we oppose. And if you really tune your ear, and get your ego out of the way, we sound just as militantly biased as Mr. Falwell and others who need to remember that God's presumptions are wider, deeper, and more challenging than their own agendas. And those agendas include, particularly, our political likes and dislikes."

Still, we are called to live, and to decide, based on those God-given moral presumptions. The least we can do is be clear about them.

All of us, because we are spiritual thinkers and actors, need to remember that George W. Bush is a child of God, duly elected under our system of laws. As such he is fallible, and he will be held accountable in the sight of God. We can and should vigorously debate the policies he and our elected representatives pursue, but if we wish to invoke a religious set of presumptions, let them be of God and not born only of our prejudices.

That seems especially important at this hour. An eminent Anglican theologian, Frederick Dennison Maurice, once famously observed that we are likely to be "right in what we affirm and wrong in what we deny."

Some of us are quick to claim the presumption against war—and it is a strong and consistent one even in the checkered history of Christianity—and equally quick to for-

get a fundamental lesson of recent history: you can't nego-
tiate with terrorists. More conservative Christians and citizens are quick to affirm the need to act before we are
wantonly attacked again, but regrettably quick to forget
that those who live by the sword are accountable before
God's judgment seat.

That's why there is renewed interest in the so-called
doctrine of the just war. This rigorous way of testing the
decision for war should, at the very least, be what we as
religious people bring to the congressional resolution and
to the facing of this hour.

Facing us at this hour is a very different world than
faced a Christian empire, whose rulers and clerics sought to
regulate war, which they saw as a given. Since Hiroshima,
many Christian thinkers have become, in effect, nuclear paci-
fists. They reason that since the nature of a weapon of mass
destruction is that it cannot be limited, the fine points of the
"just war" criteria no longer work. And since September 11
is there anyone left on the planet who thinks that war has not
been conclusively redefined? The lone terrorist seems to
stand ominously larger than the massed army.

And there is one more change on the ground, where
congregations of real people live and worship. It's a multi-
faith America in a global village, not a presumptively
Christian America in which we live and work and have our
being. My congregation recognizes this fact by offering to
our city a serious adult interfaith education program. We
recruit fine teachers from New York's best universities and
divinity schools to teach the great faith traditions to an
eager and admittedly largely ignorant audience.

A couple of years ago we had Dr. Martin Marty and Professor Jean Bethke Elshtain, both of the University of Chicago Divinity School, speaking at one of our Center of Religious Inquiry evenings. The topic was faith-based citizenship. I was struck by the friendly tension between their two positions—almost a mirror of the tensions that have existed throughout Christianity—and I was interested to read that Professor Elshtain had declined to sign a petition opposing the president's position on Iraq. Those who signed were a hundred of her fellow Christian ethicists. These one hundred represented a generally liberal spectrum of people most of us would respect and be comfortable with—a spectrum ranging from pacifist to proponent of "just war" realism.

The principles of "just war," which date to the writings of St. Augustine in the fifth century, insist that wars of aggression and aggrandizement are never acceptable. Wars may not legitimately be fought for purposes of vengeance, glory, or territorial gain. Nor should they be fought to avert dangers that are remote or that may be avoided in alternative ways. In "just war" theory, one must also consider the likelihood of success, resisting the urge to barge in and do more harm than good. Combatants must weigh carefully whether more harm will come from acting or from not acting.

It was on this basis that Dr. Elshtain refused to sign that petition because, she said, in her mind, "We who tend to weigh against war may be guilty of minimizing the threat to innocent civilians, including those who are the agreed citizens of Iraq."

There is honest tension among the most faithful and honest communities. But history and experience suggest that it is in just such a community that we struggle through to understanding and action for peace.

As Christians and as citizens, we who believe in the strong presumption for peace have work to do. "Let there be peace on earth," the old song goes, "and let it begin with me." We must learn to practice peace in our own lives and work. We must humbly acknowledge that peace work is hard work. We must take a leap of understanding to know how much more complex, how much harder, the work of peace is among nations. That should give us a little sympathy for the president and Congress and should, by grace, make us a little reluctant to settle for our own political prejudices—and to label them as irresponsible—unless and until we have done this inner work.

Then, and only then, humbly and with passion, can we insist that this brave and strong country relate with justice and generosity to our neighbors. That means having a plan that transcends raw power and self-interest. To achieve that, we must first do our inner work, our own ethical searching and deciding. Then we must be willing to work, with others so inclined, to pay attention when there is not a crisis, to build a vision of a world beyond national interest.

To build that vision, so different from the one our nation now pursues, is the work of building that earthly kingdom where the Prince of Peace reigns. For me and my people, that work begins, takes root, is tested and deepened in the real, humble ground of the local congregation.

---

1. John Calvin, *Commentaries on the Twelve Minor Prophets,* "Lecture Eighty-eighth," from the section on Micah.

Sharing a Sacred Supper: The Moral Role of a "Superpower"

DR. BEATRICE BRUTEAU

"The metaphor of the shared supper is built on the recognition that all people have absolute value, the right to 'life, liberty, and the pursuit of happiness.' We believe in the equality of all persons. This means that we must show equal respect to everyone. And that leads to sharing. If we truly acknowledge that everyone has this right to life and opportunity and we are called to respect this in real and practical ways, then sharing has to be conducted on all levels of significant human life. And the vocation of America as superpower must be to extend this value recognition and value practice worldwide. The American interest becomes the Earth interest. The superpower is responsible for the world."

—Dr. Beatrice Bruteau

Editors' note

What is it about the principle of democracy that has the potential to transform America into the provider of compassionate care for the world? How can the moral ideal of a government "of the people, by the people, and for the people" lead to the remarkable prospect of a world where the very word "superpower" will be rendered obsolete in the sharing of prosperity and responsibility by all?

Dr. Beatrice Bruteau looks back at America's original idea of the shared benefit of governing for the well-being of all citizens and wonders what would happen if that sharing of opportunity and resources were extended to the entire world. Drawing on her background as a Christian who thinks deeply about the intersection of science, philosophy, and religion as well as on her expertise in Vedanta, the study of Hindu spiritual thought, Dr. Bruteau comes up with an arrestingly simple suggestion. Let's regard the world's communities as participants in a sacred supper, she says, sharing a meal of plenty where all are welcomed regardless of wealth or status and where all are valued for their individual contributions. How would meeting at that table help to bring the good life to all people on the planet, and what will it take for America to become the chief organizer of the feast?

Sharing a Sacred Supper:
The Moral Role of a "Superpower"
Dr. Beatrice Bruteau

With power comes proportional responsibility. With unique or singular power comes a new kind of responsibility. The person or nation who wields that power can no longer use it for selfish or exclusive advantage. If Americans intend to take seriously our position of being the "only superpower," then we will have to face the question of how we think of the "American interest." Do we believe that we have the right to use our power to favor the American interest at the expense of other peoples of the world? Presently, our national officers have to take an oath that they will uphold the American interest in all situations that may affect that interest. Is that a legitimate perspective for a superpower? Or must we become obliged to care for all, without bias?

In beginning to think about this, let's start from our belief in democracy as the way people can best live together for the well-being of all. People should govern themselves for their own benefit. Originally we thought of this principle as applying to the national unit: the United States alone. What would it mean if we applied it to the world unit? Would it mean that we couldn't exploit some segments of the world for the benefit of other segments? Does democracy mean that the government "of the people, by the people" must be for all the people? For, not against?

I am going to propose that Americans, in order to be true to ourselves, to our heritage, and to the ideals that still inspire us, need to look on our life together on this planet as a sacred shared supper: sacred because it expresses our deepest values; shared because everyone is included in contributing and benefiting; and supper because it is a matter of life, meaning, joy, nourishment, and pleasure.

The American sense of the shared life began with an almost classless society. There was opportunity for everyone. There were no defined nobility. When the government was set up, it was not as a kingdom but as a republic. The power to govern was vested explicitly in the people. It is true that women, slaves, and landless people were excluded, but the power of the ideal was such that one by one these injustices were corrected—indeed, we are still working on them. But the trend is there, the value is there, and in our bones we are devoted to it.

The metaphor of the shared supper is built on the recognition that all people have absolute value, the right to "life, liberty, and the pursuit of happiness." We believe in the equality of all persons. This means that we must show equal respect to everyone. And that leads to sharing. If we truly acknowledge that everyone has this right to life and opportunity and we are called to respect this in real and practical ways, then sharing has to be conducted on all levels of significant human life. And the vocation of America as superpower must be to extend this value recognition and value practice worldwide. The American interest becomes the Earth interest. The superpower is responsible for the world.

But the very notion of "superpower" seems unfitting for the value system of the American ideal. If the moral responsibility of the superpower is to enable equality and respect and sharing, then the intention of the superpower is inevitably to attenuate and eventually to evaporate its own superior status. We are looking at our future from the beginning of a transition period. From separated nations dominated by one overpowering nation, we need to move to a level playing field of shared prosperity and responsibility.

Clearly, the first step is to practice the ideal ourselves so as to offer an example that can be helpful. That means, of course, that the counter ideals of greed and accumulation and sensationalized entertainment—the cultural aspects of the American way that do not live up to our best sense of the meaning of life—have to come under serious review, energized by this new sense of responsibility and aspiration to bring about a better world. Just as an individual, placed suddenly in a situation of new and larger responsibility—whether as a parent or as a president—will often rise to the situation, grow into the office, begin to display talents and virtues that had been mere potentialities, so a whole nation may rise to its vocation and find a new devotion to a larger work and a greater vision than it had previously known.

This means that the American people as a whole, not merely the governmental figures and their associated experts, need to engage in sober reflection on where we stand in this affair. Do we realize what the responsibility entails? Do we appreciate the responsibility that falls on each of us—that we cannot push it off onto some other entity? Reaching deep into our sense of real value, we can live as we believe is compatible with this larger scene. We must think things out, discuss our values in this position, make our views and intentions known to those who represent us. Let us have study groups and grassroots movements, a personal and political renewal. For even our democracy may be at stake if we do not practice that vigilance that the philosophers of liberty warned us to maintain.

Obviously, we must do everything we can to promote cooperation among the nations. In the first place, as with the physicians, we must do no harm. We must forsake exploitation. We must remember at all times that we are dealing with persons who have the same feelings and the same human rights that we ourselves have. We cannot operate in the world in terms of abstractions, overlooking the concrete effects on people of our theory-inspired practices. We must exhort ourselves and train ourselves to move gradually from "me first" to "all of us together." This will not come quickly or easily, but we must keep plainly in view that it has to come.

A suggestion of how to move toward the time when we will be sharing the supper more equitably may be offered in a computer game program called "Tit-for-Tat." It is famous for consistently winning prizes for producing steady cooperation more successfully than its competitors.[1] It works like this: Your initial move is to cooperate, that is, to do something helpful for the other player. If the other reciprocates, you continue to be friendly and helpful. If the other takes unfair advantage of your kindness or does something hurtful, you respond in kind—once. Then, next move, you start over again being helpful. When this behavior is repeated sufficiently, it becomes clear to both players that their individual and mutual advantage lies in being helpful rather than hurtful. Local ceasefires along the trench lines in World War I are examples, and the Marshall Plan after World War II is a major exhibit of what generosity rather than revenge can do.

Cooperation, supper sharing, evolves. Initially enlightened self-interest, it grows gently in the direction of genuine care for the other, with whom one feels more and more identification. The sense of "we" expands and becomes rooted. Americans have a good background for this. Life on the new continent gave us every opportunity to share and help one another. As the immigrants came from all over the world and inserted themselves into the dynamic of the new country, we mingled and respected one another. There are potential members of our "we" all over the planet, the one mother of us all. And Americans can open ourselves to belong to the "we" of others in return. It will take time and patience and generosity and adaptability. But it has to come. The unity and finitude of the planet dictate it.

It is always important, in urging increasing unity, to make clear that this does not, must not be taken to mean reducing everybody else to being like us. This is threatening to happen anyway, with American culture items spreading rapidly. The fruitful unity, the life-enhancing sharing, needs to preserve and encourage variety, diversity, complementarity, symbiosis. An indispensable dimension of the superpower's responsibility is to tend the symbiosis, to nurture constructive variation, to keep an eye on the balanced meal that comes to the shared table. As the symbiosis takes hold, over time and with intention and effort, the responsibility for tending and keeping an eye on will itself begin to be shared. This is the superpower's vocation—to work itself out of a job.

The shared supper gradually will take on more and more sacred aspects. It will begin with concern that basic human needs are fulfilled, and then energy and development needs. After that come community needs: social, educational, and political. This leads to sharing the very special gifts that every society has: arts and sciences and spiritual traditions, insights and teachings and aspirations. As the sharing reaches these higher levels and deeper energies of appreciation, human happiness rises. Sharing is rejoicing. From the moment of accepting the task of acting as superpower, we must keep clearly before our eyes that the bottom line, the end of all our efforts, is human happiness. All the other things that we do, we do for the sake of this universal goodness, and we are never entitled to see and to use people as means to some other end. People are the end value.

The time of confronting such a responsibility is an appropriate time to lift our eyes to the largest context in which we can see our existence. We are so used to our existence that we forget to be amazed at it—radically amazed, because it must be seen against the background of the vast universe and then against the possibility of not existing at all. How likely or unlikely are we? How significant is our presence? Maybe, with a hundred billion galaxies in our local universe, each with a hundred billion stars, many of them with planets—maybe there are other lives and other intelligences. Or maybe not so many. Perhaps, while microbial life may be even more common than we usually think, complex animal life may be relatively rare.[2] The conditions that allowed us to develop included numerous constraints and some fortuitous accidents, it seems. We may be far more wonderful than we had suspected.

What do we see when we look at the vocation and responsibility of a superpower on planet Earth in this gigantic and magical context? Does it not appear insupportably petty, ignorant, and insensitive to limit our focus to our local and immediate advantage over our copassengers on Spaceship Earth? If being the superpower is a "greatness thrust upon us," then we need to look at our responsibility in the largest scope and devote ourselves to it with the best wisdom and the most care we possess.

Life and intelligence and caring and happiness are not realities to be taken for granted. We are special. And we must take care of ourselves. We must take care of the planet. Earth is a delicately balanced set of dynamic and circulating systems. We interfere with them to our peril. Whatever nation, or combination of nations, assumes the position of superpower has by that very fact acquired the primary responsibility for the viability of the planet. If America is to live up to its obligation as the de facto superpower, we have to insist on the priority of the responsibility to protect the planet and the life that it supports. Ignoring the effects of our activities on the life-sustaining systems of earth on the grounds that protecting them would interfere with our business interests is not only morally unacceptable, it is biologically unacceptable. It is the reverse of the informed, intelligent, and trustworthy behavior that a superpower must exhibit.

This is a great call to wake up and realize what life is about. It is not an honor or a victory or a success story to be the superpower. If it has to be, then we have to shoulder it as a terribly serious task. To what do we now devote ourselves? We can't be local any longer. We have to care for the whole world. Our "oath of office" is to study and to act for the interest of the whole planet and all its creatures. And we can rise to this. We can do it.

1. Robert Axelrod, *The Evolution of Cooperation* (New York: Basic Books, 1984).

2. Peter D. Ward and Donald Brownlee, *Rare Earth: Why Complex Life Is Uncommon in the Universe* (New York: Springer, 2000).

A Source of Hope, an Instrument of Peace

ABBOT M. BASIL PENNINGTON, OSCO

"It seems to me that it is with a certain arrogance we speak of our nation as 'America.' We are but one of the nations of the Americas. We are one nation of the world, a very small world. And it is as such that we need to find our true humanity and identity. What the Creator Father has given has been given for the good of all. It must be shared by all, giving to all humans the opportunity to live a truly human life."

—Abbot M. Basil Pennington, OSCO

Editors' note

Not surprising from the monk who is best known for restoring the ancient practice of centering prayer to modern-day Christians, M. Basil Pennington stands firmly behind his statement that the Creator is the one and only superpower. From the Creator all earthly (and heavenly) power descends. Whatever power America wields owes its heritage to the founding fathers who defined our government as "one nation under God." Yet, much of the wealth and opportunity in America have been based on an economy of war. To live up to the promise of our nation's heritage, we must convert to an economy of peace.

Abbot Basil draws on his own belief in the power of hope to make a difference in people's lives, and he reminds America of its responsibility to provide that hope, not only to our own citizens but to the world. What actions must we take, for instance, to replace agricultural systems around the world that produce profitable illegal drugs with sustainable agricultural practices that would provide food for our brothers and sisters everywhere? Closer to home: How can we empty the prisons and fill the schools? Acknowledging the beneficence of our Creator and honoring our human desire for a universal community of love and peace might be a place to start.

A Source of Hope,
an Instrument of Peace
Abbot M. Basil Pennington, OSCO

To be very frank, I am not very happy about the question as it is posed. There is in truth only one superpower, and that is the power of the Creator from which all power in heaven and on earth descends and to which it all owes accountability. We may be living in a post-Christian era, certainly in a post-Christian nation, but the fact remains, as is clearly evident from the writings of our founding fathers, that this "one nation under God" was founded on principles and wisdom that have been handed down to us through the Christian heritage. That heritage proclaims: To whom more is given, from that one more is expected.

Few nations on earth have been so blessed as this fair land of ours. The natural resources are here thanks to the almighty Creator. An open-hearted immigration policy has enabled some of the world's finest minds to find a home here, and education and industry have allowed them to develop and make their contribution to the full. If these resources and this genius had been devoted to the well-being of humanity in responding to the needs of home and family and peace to the extent that they have been devoted to the works of war, this would be today a far different world. Since it enabled us to climb out of the Great Depression in the late 1930s, a war economy has been ours. We have not yet converted to an economy of peace. If every weapon in this world, biological and chemical as well as conventional and nuclear, that directly or indirectly owes its origins to our country were to disappear from the face of the earth, we would be very close to universal disarmament.

To nations that truly need humanitarian aid, how much of our foreign "aid" goes forth in the form of armaments that keep our arms factories going? If our traditional ideal of peace—an order within which women and men can live and labor together toward the realization of the good they commonly aspire to—is bartered for the economic prosperity that comes from the production and dissemination of weaponry, we have sold the heritage that gives our nation its true meaning and is a sign of hope to the whole human family.

It seems to me that it is with a certain arrogance we speak of our nation as "America." We are but one of the nations of the Americas. We are one nation of the world— a very small world. And it is as such that we need to find our true humanity and identity. What the Creator Father has given has been given for the good of all. It must be shared by all, giving to all humans the opportunity to live a truly human life.

We can hardly in any credible way stand up for the human rights of any of our sisters and brothers in other nations while with cauterized conscience we fail to render full justice to our Native Americans, from whom so much of this land has been unjustly seized, and to our African Americans, who were brought here in chains and forced to expend their lives for the development of this land. Nations far smaller than ours with far fewer resources are not marred with hordes of homeless, with multitudes who are allowed to fall between the cracks of a social system that allows the few to become exorbitantly wealthy while many cannot find meaningful employment or adequate health care. We store food supplies and pay farmers not to produce while people at home and abroad go hungry. The genius in this country with the proper political will can certainly face and respond to all these needs.

This nation was founded on the principle that every person has the God-given right to life, liberty, and the pursuit of happiness. This has been a force for vitality, growth, and development. But happiness is elusive when citizens are trapped in dehumanizing life situations; when an immense prison industry warehouses millions, depriving them of their liberty (there are more prison inmates in the state of California than in the whole of France and Germany put together) with little or no program of rehabilitation; when life is more and more unprotected at its beginnings and its completion; when the existence of the very Source of these rights is denied.

It is a difficult time to write from a spiritual perspective about America's role as a superpower when our nation teeters on the brink of undertaking, for the first time in its history, an aggressive war. When we bully the United Nations (even though our dues are far in arrears) to sanction our use of might instead of exploring with the nations the ways to build peace and cooperation, we betray our primary hope for world peace as well as our own responsibility within the human family. Smashing the Iraqi people with our mighty weapons will not redeem the humiliation we have suffered in Korea and Vietnam, the impotence we display in Colombia, where the "white weapon" that eats out the heart of our people is freely produced. We will live with the mark of Cain for having obliterated whole civilian populations in Hiroshima and Nagasaki as long as history debates whether it was only our arrogant demand for unconditional surrender that called for such a show of destructive power.

Leaders of all the religions of the world have gathered repeatedly at Assisi in a show of solidarity under the beneficent inspiration of the much-loved Poverello, St. Francis. Like him, may we seek to become an "instrument of peace." Peace can only be built on justice, a just sharing of the abundance that the Divine Goodness gives gratuitously to us all so that every human person can live a human life. If there is but one power that stands unopposed, it is time we turn from an economy of war and competition to one of peace and solidarity. Instead of using our foreign aid to arm nations, let us use it to uplift nations. It is time to stop producing weapons and start producing generators that can produce energy from the sun, wind, and water to enrich the life of the poorest of villages. It is time to send forth, instead of armed forces, an ever-growing, fully supported Peace Corps. When we destroy the fields of noxious weeds that produce the substances that are eating the heart out of our society and destroying our youth, we need to help the farmers raise other crops that can feed their people, support their life, and create a better life for all.

Every power calls forth an opposing power. While no national power or coalition of national powers is prepared to face our deadly might, a more insidious force has arisen, which has brought the destruction of war into the heart of our greatest city and has profoundly affected the lifestyle of our nation and that of the rest of the world. A single gunman with one support person was able to keep the citizens in a whole area around our national capital huddling in their homes in fear, curtailing normal life for these citizens and their children. Every power, even a so-called superpower, calls forth an opposing power *unless*, as a leader, it can align all the other powers in a united effort to bring about the realization of the common aspiration of all peoples.

The Mastery Foundation once gathered fifteen Roman Catholic and fifteen Protestant leaders from Northern Ireland. After dividing them into six groups according to religious persuasion, the Protestants were asked to list what they thought were the aims of the Catholics and the Catholics those of the Protestants. The groups were surprisingly accurate in their reports. Then each group was asked to list what were their own basic concerns. All six groups, Protestant and Catholic, came up with almost identical lists.

Our founders gave us the heritage of a vision, a hope, an expectation of people forming a government, which by its power and by its laws would foster and preserve an environment within which each person in our common equality could freely pursue his or her personal fulfillment and happiness in solidarity with neighbors. Although covered over at times by our overemphasis on material prosperity, this is basically and most fundamentally what inspires the United States and what leads immigrants to come to here. This is a vision, a hope, an expectation that accords with the deepest aspirations of every human heart. And wherever human hearts have been allowed to get in touch with this, to the extent that it actually does exist in the United States, they believe we have the power to make this a possibility for all peoples. The world today is too small for any one nation, even a nation as large and as powerful as the United States, to preserve and realize such a hope in isolation. As an eminently powerful world leader, we are challenged to foster and support the realization of this hope in every part of the human community, beginning at home but reaching out in every direction if we are to realize it at home.

This is a hope the United States has traditionally offered. A hope is not seen. It is not yet fulfilled. But it gives meaning and joy to our lives now. Without hope, what?

In the way we think, speak, and act, the United States can give hope to a world that our basic human aspirations—we might call them dreams—can and will be fulfilled. At the moment, sad to say, we seem for political reasons to foster, rather, a universal fear of terrorism.

Listen to your heart. Your own is the same as that of others. Think of sisters and brothers under one Father-Creator. Actually, our oneness in humanity is more than that. What we do to others we do to ourselves. If there is no peace in our own depths, it is because we are not peaceful in our attitude toward all our fellow humans. If there is no joy even in the midst of our affluence, it is because our fellow humans have not sufficiency and they sorrow. If there is no sense of security, it is because they are not secure but live in constant peril. Our response of threat to terrorism threatens us all. If we would reach out to our sisters and brothers with an aspiration and plan for universal well-being, the agents of terror throughout the world would no longer have any base.

Inspired by the great prophet Isaiah, let us pray that the Lord God "will destroy the veil that veils all peoples, the web that is woven over all nations" (Isaiah 23:8), setting us free to be a universal community of love. I do not want to deny the fundamental goodness of my country. I am grateful to God that it is my country. But we need to be free from the falsehoods and attachments that can lead us to betray our better selves and our fellow humans. Let us be guided by the intellect of the heart and struggle for the conditions of life in which the aspiration of every human heart for a new beginning of a better life, for resurrection, can be pursued, lived, and preserved.

The ultimate ground for this is the fact that we are, each one of us, the loving creation of a beneficent Creator who has entrusted the common stewardship of the world to us all.

Discussion Guide

Part 1—How Did We Get Here? Historical, Political, and Spiritual Perspectives

Dual Citizenship, by John Wilson

1. Wilson takes as a given that the world is tainted by sin, a theological term meaning evil—both individual and corporate—that is somehow natural to our condition as human beings. Do you agree or disagree?

2. How does your view of America's role in the world change when you believe either (a) in the basic goodness of human beings? or (b) that our most basic instincts are sinful?

From Nationalism to Patriotism: Reclaiming the American Creed, by Rev. Forrest Church

1. Church mentions many instances from American history when religious leaders have helped to guide American

nationalism and patriotism. Do you feel that religious leaders should be involved in politics today? Why or why not?

2. Do you believe that God chooses nations, or specific
groups of people, to fulfill specific roles in history?

Spiritual Reflections on America in a Global Neighborhood, by Kabir Helminski

1. Helminski chronicles some of America's changing relationships with Muslim countries throughout the twentieth century. What would you imagine to be the most
common perception of America in Muslim lands today?

2. If the world can be likened to a neighborhood, what
qualities would characterize a good neighbor country?

Called to the Task of Peacemaker, by Rev. Dr. Joan Brown Campbell

1. Campbell explains that the ideals of equality and freedom for all, outlined in the United States Constitution,
should be extended by Americans to the people of the
world. Do you agree that it is our role as a nation to do
what we can to make this happen?

2. What could or should the United States do in order to
build trust in our motives around the world?

Superpower versus Spiritual Power—Choosing Wisely, by Matthew Fox

1. Fox writes: "The spiritual is about power, about using
power well and rightly." Do you agree or disagree? Why?

2. Should spiritual people try to infuse politics, economics, and world affairs with spiritual ideals?

America Is a Light in This Dark World, by Dennis Prager

1. Prager believes strongly in the goodness that America adds to the world. In what ways do you agree?

2. What makes a country—rather than an individual person—good or bad?

Is America Losing Its Soul?, by Tony Campolo

1. Campolo identifies a lack of generosity, relative to our wealth and influence, as one of the problems with contemporary America. Do you agree or disagree? Why?

2. Would you be willing to pay more taxes in order to give more aid to countries facing medical disasters, natural disasters, poverty, hunger?

Part 2—Making Change through Our Lives

Things Are Not What They Seem to Be—Nor Are They Otherwise, by Lama Surya Das

1. Surya Das explains the Buddhist concepts of interconnectedness and karmic cause and effect. Do you believe that all people, all living things, are somehow related?

2. How would you change your everyday actions if you knew that every action of yours, no matter how subtle, had some effect in other parts of the world?

In Every Generation, Pharaoh,
by Rabbi Arthur Waskow

1. "In every generation," Waskow writes, "all human beings must see themselves as those who rise to go forth from slavery to freedom." There are those who help to free slaves and those who enslave them. Which are we?

2. How do the critical comments of others and accountability to our family, friends, and coworkers keep each of us from exercising too much power or influence over others?

Waging a Greater Jihad for America,
by Dr. Eboo Patel

1. Patel writes: "This is what we must do: Believe deeply, act boldly, begin now. Great nations are made of righteous strivings." How have the spiritual strivings of famous Americans shaped who we are today?

2. How are each of us in the midst of a "greater jihad"—a battle within, against our own lower selves?

Anger and Its Effects on Us, and the World,
by Thich Nhat Hanh

1. Thich Nhat Hanh believes that practicing mindfulness and concentration in every aspect of daily life can lead the world to peace. What does this mean? Do you agree or disagree? Why?

2. In what areas of your life do you pay very close attention to your actions and your motivations?

Part 3—*Making Change through Our Spiritual Communities*

America as an Interspiritual Superpower: A Vision to Be Realized, by Wayne Teasdale

1. Teasdale identifies a trend of "interspirituality" in America today, defined as "the phenomenon of our age of openness to other traditions of faith, wisdom, and spiritual life." Do you see this happening in your local community?

2. What can happen, in addition to increased understanding, when people become interspiritually active?

American Empire and the War against Evil, by Rosemary Radford Ruether

1. Ruether writes that prophets—similar to the prophets of the Hebrew Bible—should arise to tell us when we are on a destructive, immoral course as a nation. How would a prophet best communicate in contemporary America?

2. Whom do you see as a prophet today?

Congregation versus Superpower: The Inner Work for Peace in the Local Community of Faith, by Rev. William McD. Tully

1. Tully is committed to building what Christian theology calls an "earthly kingdom," when peace and generosity reign, and where the world at large is changed by spiritual people seeking to do what is right. How do you see the future—through the lens of your spiritual tradition?

2. How can small communities of faith affect global problems?

Sharing a Sacred Supper: The Moral Role of a "Superpower," by Dr. Beatrice Bruteau

1. "Let's regard the world's communities as participants in a sacred supper," Bruteau writes, "sharing a meal of plenty where all are welcomed regardless of wealth or status and where all are valued for their individual contributions." Do you agree or disagree that America should use its wealth in this way? Why?

2. How do you determine your own personal morality? How would you determine the correct moral decisions to make if you were president of the United States?

A Source of Hope, an Instrument of Peace, by Abbot M. Basil Pennington, OSCO

1. Pennington believes that there is only one superpower and it is not the United States. He believes that God is the only superpower in the universe. Does a basic belief that we humans are "lower than the gods," to use an old phrase, give spiritual people a common starting point?

2. What are the most important things in your life? for the life of your family? for the health of your country?

About the Contributors

Beatrice Bruteau has pioneered the integrated study of science, mathematics, philosophy, and religion. Acclaimed as an expert in Vedanta and in Catholic Christianity, Dr. Bruteau has written more than a dozen books and more than one hundred articles. Her work explores the intersection of mysticism and science and offers an alternative worldview of global community grounded in a spiritual and moral perspective. One of her most influential books is *What We Can Learn from the East;* her most recent works include *Jesus through Jewish Eyes: Rabbis and Scholars Engage an Ancient Brother in a New Conversation,* edited by Bruteau, and *Radical Optimism: Practical Spirituality in an Uncertain World.*

Joan Brown Campbell is the director of the Department of Religion at the Chautauqua Institution, a historic center for religion, the arts, and education in New York State. She was the first woman to serve as executive director of the United States office of the World Council of Churches and the first ordained woman to serve as general secretary of the

National Council of Churches. Rev. Dr. Campbell is an ordained minister in two Christian denominations, the Christian Church (Disciples of Christ) and the American Baptist Church. For more than thirty years she has been a leader in the ecumenical interfaith movement. She lectures and preaches worldwide; has led humanitarian and peace missions to South Africa, Belgrade, and the Middle East; and is published widely.

Tony Campolo is the founder and president of the Evangelical Association for the Promotion of Education, an organization that creates support programs for at-risk children in cities across the United States and Canada and is involved in educational, medical, and economic development programs in various developing countries as well. Dr. Campolo is professor emeritus of sociology at Eastern University in St. David's, Pennsylvania, and previously served for ten years on the faculty of the University of Pennsylvania. He is an ordained minister in the American Baptist Church; a media commentator on religious, social, and political issues; and the author of twenty-eight books. His most recent books are *Revolution and Renewal: How Churches Are Saving Our Cities* and *Let Me Tell You a Story: Life Lessons from Unexpected Places and Unlikely People*.

Forrest Church is senior minister of the historic All Souls Church (Unitarian Universalist) on the Upper East Side in Manhattan. Under the leadership of Rev. Dr. Church, All Souls is dedicated to being an accessible congregation, providing an environment in which all people feel welcome regardless of race, sexual orientation, or physical ability. Twenty-five social outreach programs bring the mission of All Souls into the community. Dr. Church is the author or editor of eighteen books; his addresses and opinion columns have appeared in several anthologies. He is well known for his book *Our Chosen Faith: An Introduction to Unitarian Universalism;* his most recent book is *Lifecraft: The Art of Meaning.*

Matthew Fox, a theologian, has been an ordained priest since 1967, first in the Roman Catholic Church and now in the Episcopal Church. Dr. Fox is founder and president of the University of Creation Spirituality in Oakland, California, editor in chief of *Original Blessing: A Creation Spirituality Network Newsletter*, and author of twenty-one books. Fox lectures throughout North America, Europe, and Australia on ecological and social justice, mysticism, and blessing to ever-growing audiences. His most recent books include *Creativity: Where the Divine and the Human Meet; One River, Many Wells: Wisdom Springing from Global Faiths;* and *Original Blessing: A Primer in Creation Spirituality Presented in Four Paths, Twenty-six Themes, and Two Questions.*

Kabir Helminski is a Shaikh of the Mevlevi Order and is the codirector of the Threshold Society, a nonprofit educational foundation that has developed programs to provide a structure for practice and study within Sufism and spiritual psychology. He has translated many volumes of Sufi literature, including the works of Rumi, and is the author of two books on Sufism: *Living Presence: A Sufi Way to Mindfulness and the Essential Self* and *The Knowing Heart: The Sufi Path of Transformation.* Through his work as a writer and teacher, he shares a contemporary approach to Islamic concepts and practice both within the Islamic community and outside of it. In 2001 he was the first Muslim to deliver the prestigious Wit Lectures on spirituality at Harvard Divinity School.

Thich Nhat Hanh is a Vietnamese Zen master who lives in exile in the retreat center he founded at Plum Village near Bordeaux, France. A peace activist who was nominated by Dr. Martin Luther King Jr. for the 1967 Nobel Peace Prize, Thich Nhat Hanh led the Vietnamese Buddhist Delegation to the Paris Peace Talks in 1969. Since 1983, he has lectured and led many retreats in North America and around the world on the practice of mindfulness. He is the author of more than forty books in English, including *Living Buddha, Living Christ; Peace Is Every Step: The Path of Mindfulness in Everyday Life; Being Peace; Teachings on Love;* and, most recently, *Anger: Wisdom for Cooling the Flames.*

Eboo Patel is the executive director of the Interfaith Youth Core, based in Chicago. Dr. Patel recently finished his Ph.D. in sociology at Oxford University, where he was a Rhodes scholar. The Interfaith Youth Core aims to cultivate a generation of compassionate global leaders, bringing young people of all faiths together in service to others, and helping them understand the connection between religion and social justice. In 2002, *Utne Reader* magazine named Patel one of America's "Young Visionaries Under 30." A Muslim of Indian heritage, Patel is a leader in the interfaith movement and a frequent lecturer around the world.

M. Basil Pennington, ocso, is a Cistercian monk and former abbot of Our Lady of the Holy Spirit Abbey in Georgia. He is perhaps best known for his efforts in helping the Roman Catholic Church recover its own contemplative practices, which became the centering prayer movement. The author of many modern spiritual classics, including *Centering Prayer: Renewing an Ancient Christian Prayer Form* and *Lectio Divina: Renewing the Ancient Practice of Praying the Scriptures,* Father Basil remains active in spiritual development, teaching, and writing. His most recent books include *Finding Grace at the Center: The Beginning of Centering Prayer,* coauthored with Thomas Keating, and *The Monks of Mount Athos: A Western Monk's Extraordinary Spiritual Journey on Eastern Holy Ground.*

Dennis Prager is one of America's most respected radio talk show hosts, with a weekday live broadcast from Los Angeles that is syndicated throughout the United States. He is a prolific writer of articles for journals and newspapers, a Jewish theologian, and a frequent guest on television interview shows. His writings have appeared in *Commentary,* the *Weekly Standard,* the *Wall Street Journal,* and the *Los Angeles Times.* Among his most popular books are *Happiness Is a Serious Problem: A Human Nature Repair Manual; The Nine Questions People Ask about Judaism;* and *Why the Jews? The Reason for Antisemitism.*

Rosemary Radford Ruether is Georgia Harkness Professor of Theology at Garrett-Evangelical Theological Seminary in Evanston, Illinois. Hers is an active voice for women's spirituality and she is considered one of the founders of the ecofeminism movement. Among her two dozen important and influential books are *Faith and Fratricide; Sexism and God-Talk,* a foundational text of feminist theology; *Gaia and God;* and *Women Healing Earth.* Writing with the knowledge and skill of a historian, she brings a spiritual responsibility to her work that attracts a wide readership. Her most recent book is *Women and Redemption: A Theological History.*

Lama Surya Das is one of the foremost Western Buddhist meditation teachers and scholars in the world today. Surya Das has studied Zen, Vipassana, yoga, and Tibetan Buddhism for more than thirty years. He teaches and lectures around the world, conducting many retreats and workshops each year. Working with His Holiness the Dalai Lama, Surya Das founded the Western Buddhist Teachers Network and organized conferences of Western Buddhist Meditation Teachers in Dharamsala, India. He is the author of numerous books and articles, including *Awakening the Buddha Within: Tibetan Wisdom for the Western World* and *Awakening to the Sacred: Building a Spiritual Life from Scratch.* His most recent book is *Awakening the Buddhist Heart: Integrating Love, Meaning and Connection into Every Part of Your Life.*

Wayne Teasdale is a lay monk in the Roman Catholic Church, an activist, and a teacher who combines the traditions of Christianity and Hinduism, following in the path of his teacher, Bede Griffiths. Brother Wayne is an adjunct professor at DePaul University, Columbia College, and the Catholic Theological Union, and coordinator of the Bede Griffiths International Trust. He is coeditor of *The Community of Religions* and serves on the board of trustees of the Parliament of the World's Religions. He is the author of *A Monk in the World: Cultivating a Spiritual Life* and *The Mystic Heart: Discovering a Universal Spirituality in the World's Religions*. His most recent book is *Bede Griffiths: An Introduction to His Interspiritual Thought*.

William McD. Tully is the rector of St. Bartholomew's Episcopal Church, one of New York City's great landmark churches. He is recognized throughout the mainline Christian community as a leader in renewal, based on powerful worship, extending unconditional welcome for the spiritual seeker, and passionate service to the city. St. Bart's Center for Religious Inquiry hosts interreligious programs that explore the different faith traditions in America today and encourage discussion and openness. Dr. Tully asks that all members of the community dream about the future of St. Bart's, think big, listen for God's voice, remember who and where they are and what they have to work with, and listen to the hope and pain of the city and the world.

Arthur Waskow is one of the leading creators of theory, practice, and institutions for the movement for Jewish renewal. Rabbi Waskow is the Tikkun Olam Fellow of ALEPH: Alliance for Jewish Renewal. He founded and directs the Shalom Center, a division of ALEPH that focuses on Jewish thought and practice to seek peace, pursue justice, heal the earth, and build community. Among his most recent books are *Godwrestling—Round Two: Ancient Wisdom, Future Paths* and, with Phyllis Berman, *A Time for Every Purpose Under Heaven: The Jewish Life-Spiral as a Spiritual Path*. A leader in the shaping of Jewish theology and practice committed to the protection and healing of the earth, he is also the co-editor of *Trees, Earth, and Torah: A Tu B'Shvat Anthology* and the editor of *Torah of the Earth: Exploring 4,000 Years of Ecology in Jewish Thought*, Volumes 1 and 2.

John Wilson is one of the most respected journalists, editors, and authors in Christian media today. As editor in chief of the literary review *Books & Culture* and editor-at-large for the classic Evangelical Christian weekly *Christianity Today*, Wilson is well equipped to survey the world of Christian thought in contemporary society. He is the editor of the popular and critically acclaimed anthology volumes *The Best Christian Writing 2000*, *The Best Christian Writing 2001*, and *The Best Christian Writing 2002*.

Credits

Grateful acknowledgment is given for permission from the following persons to print the material contained in this book:

"Dual Citizenship" © 2003 by John Wilson

"From Nationalism to Patriotism: Reclaiming the American Creed" © 2003 by Rev. Forrest Church

"Spiritual Reflections on America in a Global Neighborhood" © 2003 by Kabir Helminski

"Called to the Task of Peacemaker" © 2003 by Rev. Dr. Joan Brown Campbell

"Superpower versus Spiritual Power—Choosing Wisely" © 2003 by Matthew Fox

"Is America Losing Its Soul?" © 2003 by Tony Campolo

"America Is a Light in This Dark World" © 2003 by Dennis Prager

"Things Are Not What They Seem to Be—Nor Are They Otherwise" © 2003 by Lama Surya Das

"In Every Generation, Pharaoh" © 2003 by Rabbi Arthur Waskow

"Waging a Greater Jihad for America" © 2003 by Dr. Eboo Patel

"Anger and Its Effects on Us, and the World" © 2003 by Thich Nhat Hanh

"America as an Interspiritual Superpower: A Vision to Be Realized" © 2003 by Wayne Teasdale

"American Empire and the War against Evil" © 2003 by Rosemary Radford Ruether

"Congregation versus Superpower: The Inner Work for Peace in the Local Community of Faith" © 2003 by Rev. William McD. Tully

"Sharing a Sacred Supper: The Moral Role of a 'Superpower'" © 2003 by Dr. Beatrice Bruteau

"A Source of Hope, an Instrument of Peace" © 2003 by Abbot M. Basil Pennington, osco

Notes

Notes

Notes

Notes

Notes

About SKYLIGHT PATHS Publishing

SkyLight Paths Publishing is creating a place where people of different spiritual traditions come together for challenge and inspiration, a place where we can help each other understand the mystery that lies at the heart of our existence.

Through spirituality, our religious beliefs are increasingly becoming a part of our lives—rather than *apart* from our lives. While many of us may be more interested than ever in spiritual growth, we may be less firmly planted in traditional religion. Yet, we do want to deepen our relationship to the sacred, to learn from our own as well as from other faith traditions, and to practice in new ways.

SkyLight Paths sees both believers and seekers as a community that increasingly transcends traditional boundaries of religion and denomination—people wanting to learn from each other, *walking together, finding the way.*

We at SkyLight Paths take great care to produce beautiful books that present meaningful spiritual content in a form that reflects the art of making high quality books. Therefore, we want to acknowledge those who contributed to the production of this book.

PRODUCTION
Tim Holtz & Martha McKinney

EDITORIAL
Amanda Dupuis, Maura D. Shaw & Emily Wichland

COVER AND TEXT DESIGN
Tim Holtz

PRINTING & BINDING
Versa Press, East Peoria, Illinois

Spirituality

Who Is My God?
An Innovative Guide to Finding Your Spiritual Identity
Created by *the Editors at SkyLight Paths*

Spiritual Type™ + Tradition Indicator = Spiritual Identity

Your Spiritual Identity is an undeniable part of who you are—whether you've thought much about it or not. This dynamic resource provides a helpful framework to begin or deepen your spiritual growth. Start by taking the unique Spiritual Identity Self-Test™; tabulate your results; then explore one, two, or more of twenty-eight faiths/spiritual paths followed in America today. "An innovative and entertaining way to think—and rethink—about your own spiritual path, or perhaps even to find one." —Dan Wakefield, author of *How Do We Know When It's God?*
6 x 9, 160 pp, Quality PB, ISBN 1-893361-08-X **$15.95**

Spiritual Manifestos: *Visions for Renewed Religious Life in America from Young Spiritual Leaders of Many Faiths*
Edited by *Niles Elliot Goldstein*; Preface by *Martin E. Marty*

Discover the reasons why so many people have kept organized religion at arm's length.

Here, ten young spiritual leaders, most in their mid-thirties, representing the spectrum of religious traditions—Protestant, Catholic, Jewish, Buddhist, Unitarian Universalist—present the innovative ways they are transforming our spiritual communities and our lives. "These ten articulate young spiritual leaders engender hope for the vitality of 21st-century religion." —Forrest Church, Minister of All Souls Church in New York City
6 x 9, 256 pp, HC, ISBN 1-893361-09-8 **$21.95**

  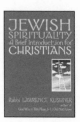 

Jewish Spirituality: *A Brief Introduction for Christians*
by *Lawrence Kushner*

Lawrence Kushner, whose award-winning books have brought Jewish spirituality to life for countless readers of all faiths and backgrounds, tailors his unique style to address Christians' questions, revealing the essence of Judaism in a way that people whose own tradition traces its roots to Judaism can understand and enjoy.
5½ x 8½, 112 pp, Quality PB, ISBN 1-58023-150-0 **$12.95**

The Geography of Faith
Underground Conversations on Religious, Political and Social Change
by *Daniel Berrigan* and *Robert Coles*; Updated introduction and afterword by the authors

A classic of faith-based activism—updated for a new generation.

Listen in on the conversations between these two great teachers—one a renegade priest wanted by the FBI for his protests against the Vietnam war, the other a future Pulitzer Prize-winning journalist—as they struggle with what it means to put your faith to the test. Discover how their story of challenging the status quo during a time of great political, religious, and social change is just as applicable to our lives today. 6 x 9, 224 pp, Quality PB, ISBN 1-893361-40-3 **$16.95**

Spiritual Biography

The Life of Evelyn Underhill
An Intimate Portrait of the Groundbreaking Author of Mysticism
by *Margaret Cropper*; Foreword by *Dana Greene*

Evelyn Underhill was a passionate writer and teacher who wrote elegantly on mysticism, worship, and devotional life. This is the story of how she made her way toward spiritual maturity, from her early days of agnosticism to the years when her influence was felt throughout the world. 6 x 9, 288 pp, 5 b/w photos, Quality PB, ISBN 1-893361-70-5 **$18.95**

Zen Effects: *The Life of Alan Watts*
by *Monica Furlong*

The first and only full-length biography of one of the most charismatic spiritual leaders of the twentieth century—now back in print!

Through his widely popular books and lectures, Alan Watts (1915–1973) did more to introduce Eastern philosophy and religion to Western minds than any figure before or since. Here is the only biography of this charismatic figure, who served as Zen teacher, Anglican priest, lecturer, academic, entertainer, a leader of the San Francisco renaissance, and author of more than 30 books, including *The Way of Zen, Psychotherapy East and West* and *The Spirit of Zen.* 6 x 9, 264 pp, Quality PB, ISBN 1-893361-32-2 **$16.95**

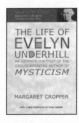   

Simone Weil: *A Modern Pilgrimage*
by *Robert Coles*

The extraordinary life of the spiritual philosopher who's been called both saint and madwoman.

The French writer and philosopher Simone Weil (1906–1943) devoted her life to a search for God—while avoiding membership in organized religion. Robert Coles' intriguing study of Weil details her short, eventful life, and is an insightful portrait of the beloved and controversial thinker whose life and writings influenced many (from T. S. Eliot to Adrienne Rich to Albert Camus), and continue to inspire seekers everywhere. 6 x 9, 208 pp, Quality PB, ISBN 1-893361-34-9 **$16.95**

Inspired Lives: *Exploring the Role of Faith and Spirituality in the Lives of Extraordinary People*
by *Joanna Laufer* and *Kenneth S. Lewis*

Contributors include *Ang Lee, Wynton Marsalis, Kathleen Norris, Hakeem Olajuwon, Christopher Parkening, Madeleine L'Engle, Doc Watson,* and many more

In this moving book, soul-searching conversations unearth the importance of spirituality and personal faith for more than forty artists and innovators who have made a real difference in our world through their work. 6 x 9, 256 pp, Quality PB, ISBN 1-893361-33-0 **$16.95**

Spiritual Practice

Women Pray
Voices through the Ages, from Many Faiths, Cultures, and Traditions
Edited and with introductions by *Monica Furlong*

Many ways—new and old—to communicate with the Divine.

This beautiful gift book celebrates the rich variety of ways women around the world have called out to the Divine—with words of joy, praise, gratitude, wonder, petition, longing, and even anger—from the ancient world up to our own time. Prayers from women of nearly every religious or spiritual background give us an eloquent expression of what it means to communicate with God. 5 x7¼,256 pp, Deluxe HC with ribbon marker, ISBN 1-893361-25-X **$19.95**

Praying with Our Hands: *Twenty-One Practices of Embodied Prayer from the World's Spiritual Traditions*
by *Jon M. Sweeney*; Photographs by *Jennifer J. Wilson*;
Foreword by *Mother Tessa Bielecki*; Afterword by *Taitetsu Unno, Ph.D.*

A spiritual guidebook for bringing prayer into our bodies.

This inspiring book of reflections and accompanying photographs shows us twenty-one simple ways of using our hands to speak to God, to enrich our devotion and ritual. All express the various approaches of the world's religious traditions to bringing the body into worship. Spiritual traditions represented include Anglican, Sufi, Zen, Roman Catholic, Yoga, Shaker, Hindu, Jewish, Pentecostal, Eastern Orthodox, and many others.
8 x 8, 96 pp, 22 duotone photographs, Quality PB, ISBN 1-893361-16-0 **$16.95**

   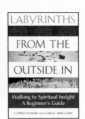

The Sacred Art of Listening
Forty Reflections for Cultivating a Spiritual Practice
by *Kay Lindahl*; Illustrations by *Amy Schnapper*

More than ever before, we need to embrace the skills and practice of listening. You will learn to: Speak clearly from your heart • Communicate with courage and compassion • Heighten your awareness for deep listening • Enhance your ability to listen to people with different belief systems. 8 x 8, 160 pp, Illus., Quality PB, ISBN 1-893361-44-6 **$16.95**

Labyrinths from the Outside In
Walking to Spiritual Insight—a Beginner's Guide
by *Donna Schaper* and *Carole Ann Camp*

The user-friendly, interfaith guide to making and using labyrinths—for meditation, prayer, and celebration.

Labyrinth walking is a spiritual exercise *anyone* can do. This accessible guide unlocks the mysteries of the labyrinth for all of us, providing ideas for using the labyrinth walk for prayer, meditation, and celebrations to mark the most important moments in life. Includes instructions for making a labyrinth of your own and finding one in your area.
6 x 9, 208 pp, b/w illus. and photographs, Quality PB, ISBN 1-893361-18-7 **$16.95**

SkyLight Illuminations Series
Andrew Harvey, series editor

Offers today's spiritual seeker an enjoyable entry into the great classic texts of the world's spiritual traditions. Each classic is presented in an accessible translation, with facing pages of guided commentary from experts, giving you the keys you need to understand the history, context, and meaning of the text. This series enables readers of all backgrounds to experience and understand classic spiritual texts directly, and to make them a part of their lives. Andrew Harvey writes the foreword to each volume, an insightful, personal introduction to each classic.

Bhagavad Gita: *Annotated & Explained*
Translation by *Shri Purohit Swami;* Annotation by *Kendra Crossen Burroughs*

"The very best Gita for first-time readers." —Ken Wilber

Millions of people turn daily to India's most beloved holy book, whose universal appeal has made it popular with non-Hindus and Hindus alike. This edition introduces you to the characters; explains references and philosophical terms; shares the interpretations of famous spiritual leaders and scholars; and more. 5½ x 8½, 192 pp, Quality PB, ISBN 1-893361-28-4 **$16.95**

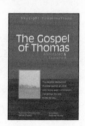

The Way of a Pilgrim: *Annotated & Explained*
Translation and annotation by *Gleb Pokrovsky*

The classic of Russian spirituality—now with facing-page commentary that illuminates and explains the text for you.

This delightful account is the story of one man who sets out to learn the prayer of the heart—also known as the "Jesus prayer"—and how the practice transforms his existence. This edition guides you through an abridged version of the text with facing-page annotations explaining the names, terms and references. 5½ x 8½, 160 pp, Quality PB, ISBN 1-893361-31-4 **$14.95**

The Gospel of Thomas: *Annotated & Explained*
Translation and annotation by *Stevan Davies*

The recently discovered mystical sayings of Jesus—now with facing-page commentary that illuminates and explains the text for you.

Discovered in 1945, this collection of aphoristic sayings sheds new light on the origins of Christianity and the intriguing figure of Jesus, portraying the Kingdom of God as a present fact about the world, rather than a future promise or future threat. This edition guides you through the text with annotations that focus on the meaning of the sayings, ideal for readers with no previous background in Christian history or thought.
5½ x 8½, 192 pp, Quality PB, ISBN 1-893361-45-4 **$15.95**

SkyLight Illuminations Series
Andrew Harvey, series editor

Zohar: *Annotated & Explained*
Translation and annotation by *Daniel C. Matt*

The cornerstone text of Kabbalah, now with facing-page commentary that illuminates and explains the text for you.

The best-selling author of *The Essential Kabbalah* brings together in one place the most important teachings of the *Zohar*, the canonical text of Jewish mystical tradition. Guides readers step by step through the midrash, mystical fantasy and Hebrew scripture that make up the *Zohar*, explaining the inner meanings in facing-page commentary. Ideal for readers without any prior knowledge of Jewish mysticism.
5½ x 8½, 176 pp, Quality PB, ISBN 1-893361-51-9 **$15.95**

Selections from the Gospel of Sri Ramakrishna
Annotated & Explained
Translation by *Swami Nikhilananda*; Annotation by *Kendra Crossen Burroughs*

The words of India's greatest example of God-consciousness and mystical ecstasy in recent history—now with facing-page commentary that illuminates and explains the text for you.

Introduces the fascinating world of the Indian mystic and the universal appeal of his message that has inspired millions of devotees for more than a century. Selections from the original text and insightful yet unobtrusive commentary highlight the most important and inspirational teachings. Ideal for readers without any prior knowledge of Hinduism.
5½ x 8½, 240 pp, b/w photographs, Quality PB, ISBN 1-893361-46-2 **$16.95**

Dhammapada: *Annotated & Explained*
Translation by *Max Müller* and revised by *Jack Maguire*; Annotation by *Jack Maguire*

The classic of Buddhist spiritual practice—now with facing-page commentary that illuminates and explains the text for you.

The Dhammapada—words spoken by the Buddha himself over 2,500 years ago—is notoriously difficult to understand for the first-time reader. Now you can experience it with understanding even if you have no previous knowledge of Buddhism. Enlightening facing-page commentary explains all the names, terms, and references, giving you deeper insight into the text. An excellent introduction to Buddhist life and practice.
5½ x 8½, 160 pp, Quality PB, ISBN 1-893361-42-X **$14.95**

Meditation/Prayer

Finding Grace at the Center: *The Beginning of Centering Prayer*
by *M. Basil Pennington, OCSO, Thomas Keating, OCSO,* and *Thomas E. Clarke, SJ*

The book that helped launch the Centering Prayer "movement." Explains the prayer of *The Cloud of Unknowing,* posture and relaxation, the three simple rules of centering prayer, and how to cultivate centering prayer throughout all aspects of your life.
5 x 7¼,112 pp, HC, ISBN 1-893361-69-1 **$14.95**

Three Gates to Meditation Practice
A Personal Journey into Sufism, Buddhism, and Judaism
by *David A. Cooper*

> Shows us how practicing within more than one spiritual tradition can lead us to our true home.

Here are over fifteen years from the journey of "post-denominational rabbi" David A. Cooper, author of *God Is a Verb,* and his wife, Shoshana—years in which the Coopers explored a rich variety of practices, from chanting Sufi *dhikr* to Buddhist Vipassanā meditation, to the study of Kabbalah and esoteric Judaism. Their experience demonstrates that the spiritual path is really completely within our reach, whoever we are, whatever we do—as long as we are willing to practice it. 5½ x 8½, 240 pp, Quality PB, ISBN 1-893361-22-5 **$16.95**

 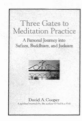  

Silence, Simplicity & Solitude
A Complete Guide to Spiritual Retreat at Home
by *David A. Cooper*

> The classic personal spiritual retreat guide that enables readers to create their own self-guided spiritual retreat at home.

Award-winning author David Cooper traces personal mystical retreat in all of the world's major traditions, describing the varieties of spiritual practices for modern spiritual seekers. Cooper shares the techniques and practices that encompass the personal spiritual retreat experience, allowing readers to enhance their meditation practices and create an effective, self-guided spiritual retreat in their own homes—without the instruction of a meditation teacher. 5½ x 8½, 336 pp, Quality PB, ISBN 1-893361-04-7 **$16.95**

Prayer for People Who Think Too Much
A Guide to Everyday, Anywhere Prayer from the World's Faith Traditions
by *Mitch Finley*

> Helps us make prayer a natural part of daily living.

Takes a thoughtful look at how each major faith tradition incorporates prayer into *daily* life. Explores Christian sacraments, Jewish holy days, Muslim daily prayer, "mindfulness" in Buddhism, and more, to help you better understand and enhance your own prayer practices. "I love this book." —Caroline M. Myss, Ph.D., author of *Anatomy of the Spirit*
5½ x 8½, 224 pp, Quality PB, ISBN 1-893361-21-7 **$16.95**; HC, ISBN 1-893361-00-4 **$21.95**

Kabbalah

Honey from the Rock
An Introduction to Jewish Mysticism
by *Lawrence Kushner*

An insightful and absorbing introduction to the ten gates of Jewish mysticism and how it applies to daily life. "The easiest introduction to Jewish mysticism you can read."
6 x 9, 176 pp, Quality PB, ISBN 1-58023-073-3 **$15.95**

Eyes Remade for Wonder
The Way of Jewish Mysticism and Sacred Living
A Lawrence Kushner Reader
Intro. by *Thomas Moore*, author of *Care of the Soul*

Whether you are new to Kushner or a devoted fan, you'll find inspiration here. With samplings from each of Kushner's works, and a generous amount of new material, this book is to be read and reread, each time discovering deeper layers of meaning in our lives.
6 x 9, 240 pp, Quality PB, ISBN 1-58023-042-3 **$18.95**; HC, ISBN 1-58023-014-8 **$23.95**

Invisible Lines of Connection
Sacred Stories of the Ordinary
by *Lawrence Kushner* **AWARD WINNER!**

Through his everyday encounters with family, friends, colleagues and strangers, Kushner takes us deeply into our lives, finding flashes of spiritual insight in the process.
5½ x 8½, 160 pp, Quality PB, ISBN 1-879045-98-2 **$15.95**

  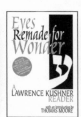  

Finding Joy
A Practical Spiritual Guide to Happiness
by *Dannel I. Schwartz* with *Mark Hass* **AWARD WINNER!**

Explains how to find joy through a time honored, creative—and surprisingly practical—approach based on the teachings of Jewish mysticism and Kabbalah.
6 x 9, 192 pp, Quality PB, ISBN 1-58023-009-1 **$14.95**; HC, ISBN 1-879045-53-2 **$19.95**

Ancient Secrets
Using the Stories of the Bible to Improve Our Everyday Lives
by *Rabbi Levi Meier, Ph.D.* **AWARD WINNER!**

Drawing on a broad range of wisdom writings, distinguished rabbi and psychologist Levi Meier takes a thoughtful, wise and fresh approach to showing us how to apply the stories of the Bible to our everyday lives.
5½ x 8½, 288 pp, Quality PB, ISBN 1-58023-064-4 **$16.95**

Children's Spirituality

Becoming Me: *A Story of Creation*
by *Martin Boroson*
Full-color illus. by *Christopher Gilvan-Cartwright*

For ages 4 & up

Told in the personal "voice" of the Creator, here is a story about creation and relationship that is about each one of us. In simple words and with radiant illustrations, the Creator tells an intimate story about love, about friendship and playing, about our world—and about ourselves. And with each turn of the page, we're reminded that we just might be closer to our Creator than we think!

8 x 10, 32 pp, Full-color illus., HC, ISBN 1-893361-11-X **$16.95**

  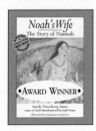

Noah's Wife
The Story of Naamah
by *Sandy Eisenberg Sasso*
Full-color illus. by *Bethanne Andersen*

For ages 4 & up

This new story, based on an ancient text, opens readers' religious imaginations to new ideas about the well-known story of the Flood. When God tells Noah to bring the animals of the world onto the ark, God also calls on Naamah, Noah's wife, to save each plant on Earth. "A lovely tale.... Children of all ages should be drawn to this parable for our times." —Tomie de Paola, artist/author of books for children
9 x 12, 32 pp, HC, Full-color illus., ISBN 1-58023-134-9 **$16.95**

In God's Name
by *Sandy Eisenberg Sasso*; Full-color illus. by *Phoebe Stone*

For ages 4 & up

Like an ancient myth in its poetic text and vibrant illustrations, this award-winning modern fable about the search for God's name celebrates the diversity and, at the same time, the unity of all the people of the world.
9 x 12, 32 pp, HC, Full-color illus., ISBN 1-879045-26-5 **$16.95**

Also available in Spanish:
El nombre de Dios 9 x 12, 32 pp, HC, Full-color illus., ISBN 1-893361-63-2 **$16.95**

The 11th Commandment
Wisdom from Our Children
by *The Children of America*

For ages 4 & up

"If there were an Eleventh Commandment, what would it be?" Children of many religious denominations across America answer this question—in their own drawings and words. "A rare book of spiritual celebration for all people, of all ages, for all time." —*Bookviews*
8 x 10, 48 pp, HC, Full-color illus., ISBN 1-879045-46-X **$16.95**

Children's Spirituality

Ten Amazing People
And How They Changed the World

For ages 6–10

by *Maura D. Shaw*; Foreword by *Dr. Robert Coles*
Full-color illus. by *Stephen Marchesi*

Black Elk • Dorothy Day • Malcolm X • Mahatma Gandhi •
Martin Luther King, Jr. • Mother Teresa • Janusz Korczak •
Desmond Tutu • Thich Nhat Hanh • Albert Schweitzer

This vivid, inspirational, and authoritative book will open new possibilities for children by telling the stories of how ten of the past century's greatest leaders changed the world in important ways.

8½ x 11, 48 pp, HC, Full-color illus., ISBN 1-893361-47-0 **$17.95**

A New Series: What You Will See Inside ...

This important new series of books is designed to show children ages 6–10 the Who, What, When, Where, Why and How of traditional houses of worship, liturgical celebrations, and rituals of different world faiths, empowering them to respect and understand their own religious traditions—and those of their friends and neighbors.

What You Will See Inside a Catholic Church

For ages 6–10

by *Reverend Michael Keane*; Foreword by *Robert J. Keeley, Ed.D.*
Full-color photographs by *Aaron Pepis*

A colorful, fun-to-read introduction to the traditions of Catholic worship and faith. Visually and informatively explains the common use of the altar, processional cross, baptismal font, votive candles, and more.

8½ x 10½, 32 pp, HC, ISBN 1-893361-54-3 **$17.95**

Also available in Spanish:
Lo que se puede ver dentro de una iglesia católica
8½ x 10½, 32 pp, HC, ISBN 1-893361-66-7 **$16.95**

What You Will See Inside a Mosque

For ages 6–10

by *Aisha Karen Khan*; Foreword by *Dr. Sayyid M. Syeed*
Full-color photographs by *Aaron Pepis*

Full-page photographs set the scene for this fun and informative introduction to the who, what, when, why, and how of Muslim faith and worship. Clearly identifies and explains everything from the *qibla* to how people prepare to pray to the Five Pillars of Islam and what they mean in people's everyday lives.

8½ x 10½, 32 pp, HC, ISBN 1-893361-60-8 **$16.95**

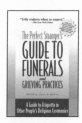

Spirituality

Journeys of Simplicity
Traveling Light with Thomas Merton, Bashō, Edward Abbey, Annie Dillard & Others
by *Philip Harnden*

There is a more graceful way of traveling through life.

Offers vignettes of forty "travelers" and the few ordinary things they carried with them—from place to place, from day to day, from birth to death. What Thoreau took to Walden Pond. What Thomas Merton packed for his final trip to Asia. What Annie Dillard keeps in her writing tent. What an impoverished cook served M. F. K. Fisher for dinner. Much more.

"'How much should I carry with me?' is the quintessential question for any journey, especially the journey of life. Herein you'll find sage, sly, wonderfully subversive advice."
—Bill McKibben, author of *The End of Nature* and *Enough*
5 x 7¼, 128 pp, HC, ISBN 1-893361-76-4 **$16.95**

The Alphabet of Paradise
An A–Z of Spirituality for Everyday Life
by *Howard Cooper*

"An extraordinary book." —Karen Armstrong

One of the most eloquent new voices in spirituality, Howard Cooper takes us on a journey of discovery—into ourselves and into the past—to find the signposts that can help us live more meaningful lives. In twenty-six engaging chapters—from A to Z—Cooper spiritually illuminates the subjects of daily life, using an ancient Jewish mystical method of interpretation that reveals both the literal and more allusive meanings of each. Topics include: Awe, Bodies, Creativity, Dreams, Emotions, Sports, and more.
5 x 7¼, 224 pp, Quality PB, ISBN 1-893361-80-2 **$16.95**

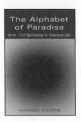

Winter
A Spiritual Biography of the Season
Edited by *Gary Schmidt* and *Susan M. Felch*; Illustrations by *Barry Moser*

Explore how the dormancy of winter can be a time of spiritual preparation and transformation.

In thirty stirring pieces, *Winter* delves into the varied feelings that winter conjures in us, calling up both the barrenness and the beauty of the natural world in wintertime. Includes selections by Will Campbell, Rachel Carson, Annie Dillard, Donald Hall, Ron Hansen, Jane Kenyon, Jamaica Kincaid, Barry Lopez, Kathleen Norris, John Updike, E. B. White, and many others.

"This outstanding anthology features top-flight nature and spirituality writers on the fierce, inexorable season of winter.... Remarkably lively and warm, despite the icy subject."
—★*Publishers Weekly* Starred Review
6 x 9, 288 pp, 6 b/w illus., HC, ISBN 1-893361-53-5 **$21.95**